Praise for *Ali's Well That Ends Well*

"You know I love a funny woman who can be so candid, honest, and poignant—and still make me laugh!"   —Busy Phillips

"Only Ali can mine the humor and poignancy of a pandemic. It is so insightful and so damn funny! I want to go clamming with her!"   —Molly Shannon

"In the latest installment of her bestselling life-as-Ali chronicles, *Ali's Well That Ends Well*, Ali Wentworth takes us once again into her delightful and dizzying world. But this time we get right into bed with her—her *sick* bed, that is—as she battles aches, fears, and lockdown-delirium as an early victim of Covid. But in Ali's hilariously deft hands, the frightening ordeal is braided with thoughtful life lessons. I loved this book."—Marlo Thomas

"Wentworth strikes gold in this hilarious, touching, and wonderfully frank look at her life during the first year of the Covid-19 pandemic. . . . Throughout, Wentworth delivers her quips and quibbles with a perceptive insight that's sure to keep fans entertained while knowingly nodding their heads. Life for Wentworth is one big adventure; and lucky for readers, she brings them along for the ride."   —*Publishers Weekly* (starred review)

"Laugh-out-loud. . . . A light, amusing work for fans of Wentworth's quirky sense of humor."   —*Kirkus Reviews*

Praise for *Happily Ali After*

"Hilarious. . . . Her glass isn't half full—it's 'empty and cracked.'"   —*Entertainment Weekly* (Must List)

"Razor-sharp."   *—Cosmopolitan*

"[A] collection of essays in Wentworth's acerbic, bawdy voice. . . .
Wentworth makes for great company."   *—Elle*

"Irresistible. . . . She is sharply observant and incisively funny. . . .
Readers who like Nora Ephron and Laurie Notaro won't want
to miss Wentworth. Reading this book is like sitting with a best
girlfriend—how fitting it is that Wentworth dedicated it to all
of hers."   *—Library Journal*

"Wentworth is funny. She gracefully and elegantly bares embarrassing stories from her past and hilariously conveys the chal-
lenges of her marriage . . . and of raising their two children. . . .
With wit, the author may inspire others to simply enjoy the moment and not let themselves get in the way."   *Kirkus Reviews*

"Wentworth spins hilarious tales of parenting, relationships, and,
yes, getting older."   *—People*

Praise for *Ali in Wonderland*

"Hilarious."   *—Marie Claire*

"Everything that comes out of Ali Wentworth's mouth is
funny!"   —Jerry Seinfeld

"Ali Wentworth's book is like *Chicken Soup for the Vagina*. Gays
and straight men, I'm not leaving you out here! Ali is truly one
of the quickest, funniest girls I've ever met. Enjoy!"

—Kathy Griffin

"Ali has written a truly hilarious book . . . and she's also a good
kisser!"   —Chelsea Handler

Ali's
Well
That
Ends
Well

ALSO BY ALI WENTWORTH

Go Ask Ali

Happily Ali After

Ali in Wonderland

The WASP Cookbook

Tales of Desperation and a Little Inspiration

Ali's Well That Ends Well

ALI WENTWORTH

HARPER

NEW YORK · LONDON · TORONTO · SYDNEY

HARPER

ALI'S WELL THAT ENDS WELL. Copyright © 2022 by Alexandra Wentworth. All rights reserved. Printed in the United States of America. No part of this book may be used or reproduced in any manner whatsoever without written permission except in the case of brief quotations embodied in critical articles and reviews. For information, address HarperCollins Publishers, 195 Broadway, New York, NY 10007.

HarperCollins books may be purchased for educational, business, or sales promotional use. For information, please email the Special Markets Department at SPsales@harpercollins.com.

FIRST HARPER PAPERBACKS EDITION PUBLISHED 2023.

Designed by Bonni Leon-Berman

Library of Congress Cataloging-in-Publication Data has been applied for.

ISBN 978-0-06-298087-8 (pbk.)

23 24 25 26 27 LBC 5 4 3 2 1

If you're reading this book, it's dedicated to you.

Most of these stories are true. Okay, maybe I embellished a little. But at least I gave everyone better names!

Things are going to get a lot worse before they get worse.

—LILY TOMLIN

CONTENTS

Ali's
Well
That
Ends
Well

I Got It

Cooper, my rescue hound mix, has a habit of running away. All hounds are ruled by scent. If he caught a whiff of hot dog, he would run through a plateglass door—like a cheetah, he would keep going for thousands of miles regardless of cars, tar pits, or frozen terrain. His DNA kicks in at the thought of a wounded woodland creature hopping nearby. Or steak. And like all hound dogs and most hormonal teenage boys, he makes bad decisions.

One frigid March afternoon, I took Cooper to the beach to exhaust him. An impossible feat. As I stated, this dog could sprint from Cape Cod to San Francisco, stopping only to pee on a trash can or a stranger's leg. And then he would jump up and down like a winner on *The Price Is Right* to do it all again. He brings me an incredible amount of unconditional love (when I feed him) and emotional support (when he's in an enclosed environment). But when his soundtrack is

"Fly Like an Eagle," he can cause me a tremendous amount of distress.

We had just made it down the sandy path to the dunes when Cooper froze. Right paw up. Gaze straight ahead. A statue. Beat. Beat. Beat. And then he took off, spraying sand in his wake. In a matter of seconds, he was a black speck in the distance racing a seagull one hundred feet in the air above him.

My ears ached, and my cheeks burned in the bitter wind. "Cooper!" I screamed into a chilly vacuum. I trudged toward him. My Ugg boots were so heavy. I felt like Ninoshka of the North.

"Cooooooppppppeerrrr!" I yelled again.

I was suddenly aware of my breath, or lack thereof. I could not take in a full, deep breath. Not that I ever climbed Everest (or the stairs in the subway, for that matter), but I was conscious of a lack of oxygen. I assumed it was the weather. Or that bully in my head who whispers, *You're old and out of shape.* I pushed away that ridiculous thought as I marched on. Was it possible the sand had gotten *thicker*?

I felt like a ninety-year-old woman with emphysema. Okay, I'm not a skeletal New Yorker who lives on skinned green apples and SoulCycle, but the fact that I couldn't hoist my ass up a two-foot dune was upsetting.

"Cooper!!!!!! Come . . ." My voice trailed off.

Damnit. I felt weak. Like the beloved Beth in *Little*

Women. The beach was empty. Why wouldn't it be? It was a wretched afternoon that felt like the prologue to the film *Fargo*. A day that only stoned teenagers or heartbroken widows come out for. I suddenly had the frightening thought that I had become so winded I would pass out. The rising tide would pull me into the surf, and I would disappear into the crashing waves, swept out to sea. Gone forever without a trace. Because my fucking dog had decided that a seagull, which was impossible to catch, was worth chasing for five miles. They would have to punch that up for my obituary.

So I sank down into the wet, gritty sand and prayed Cooper would make his way back to me before I became shark chum. I hoisted my down coat over my head and buried my face in my hands. Even when I was motionless, my breathing was labored. I was the soundtrack to the anti-smoking commercials with sad people hooked up to oxygen machines, gasping for air. Which wasn't such a far-fetched image given that I smoked a pack of cigarettes a day for twenty years.

A slimy nose nudged my back. I jumped. Not that serial killers scour abandoned beaches in late winter . . . but I had just watched the Ted Bundy tapes on Netflix.

"Cooper!" He was soaked, slimy, and had that fetid stink which could only mean he had rolled in dead fish. Someday I would like to meet a scientist or biological behaviorist who can explain two things about the animal kingdom that I just can't fathom. One—how a boa constrictor can swallow a deer whole. And two—why my dog feels the need to baste himself in anything dead, rotting, or defecated. What other dog is going to take a whiff of that and want to make puppies?

Thank God, we could go home. I untied the leash from my waist and secured it on his collar. I couldn't risk Cooper taking flight after another bird. It was freezing. I was starving. I'd only had a glop of raw cookie dough and a cinnamon doughnut for breakfast (maybe that's why I couldn't walk far?) and the wheezing was becoming louder. Could a piece of doughnut have gotten lodged in my lung? Is that even possible?

As I staggered up the path to the parking lot, I promised myself I was going to start eating mostly plants—no more sugar!—and join a Broadway musical dance class. Sure, I was middle-aged on paper, but I was convinced I could turn back time with a healthy new regime of green smoothies. I wished I was more obsessed with my looks. I wish I were born with that chip that makes one cry at the mere sight of cellulite or go on spirulina-and-bone-broth fasts that allow me to shit twenty pounds in a single hour. My husband probably wishes he could buy that chip on Amazon for me.

There was something about my labored breathing that had me concerned, though. Ego aside, it just didn't feel normal.

Cooper pluckily jumped into the car, no doubt antici-pating his next adventure in the grassy backyard, where the squirrels declared war on him every single day, throwing nuts and Cirque du Soleiling through the pine trees to taunt him. But he loves it. And runs, frothing at the mouth, secure in the knowledge that someday a squirrel will lose its grip and tumble into his jaws.

I blasted the heat and turned on NPR. I couldn't tell which of us was breathing (or barking) harder. At least he had an excuse, having run five miles in less than twenty minutes. Starting Monday I would embark on a rigorous workout regimen. I would row or climb or run and pick up huge kettleballs or -bells and lunge. Every woman I know who has an enviable body does lunges.

My mind quickly meandered to its favorite distraction: dinner. In cold weather, food needed to be draped in a blan-ket of sauce. Tonight felt like a roast-chicken-with-parsnips kind of night. It was healthy. Except for the part where I boiled the parsnips in heavy cream.

When we reached the house Cooper started scratching at the car window. Just in case there was a deer or a basket of baby rabbits waiting for him in the backyard. He has a habit of jumping over me before the car has completely stopped, digging his nails into my thighs as he vaults across my lap. But this time he just sat panting in the passenger seat. I sat too. Trying to find air. I couldn't muster the fortitude to skip into the house like a hypercaffeinated Mary Poppins and whip up a magical evening as usual. I still couldn't breathe properly. So there Cooper and I sat. In a muddy Mini Cooper, listening to the chirping of birds as dusk settled in.

It didn't even occur to me that I had contracted the deadly virus that was making its way around the world and bringing the global economy to its knees. At that point, it was just this deviant thing you read about in the news that seemed unfathomable. Like fascism.

I called my husband and left a message. "I can't breathe very well . . . I think I might be getting bronchitis." Perhaps this was my punishment for smoking Kool menthol cigarettes in boarding school so as not to be bullied by the mean girls, but since I'd quit smoking twenty years ago, my relationship with my lungs has been fraught. I've had pneumonia a few times and am on an annual bronchitis cycle. On my birthday in January, I usually fall prey to a week in bed hocking up green phlegm and pleading for Mucinex and chicken soup. Extra matzo balls. But this was March! I hoped my husband wouldn't play the *you need to get healthy* card. He's so kind to me and yet so vindictive about my immune system. He always wins with that. Mostly because he's the fittest, healthiest person I know. He knows how to swing a kettleball. Or -bell. Whatever those things are in the basement that I can't move and once tried to use as a doorstop.

I collapsed on my bed, still trying to steady my breathing. I zoned out on an episode of *Black-ish*. George called me back. "You need to get tested." *That's ridiculous*, I thought. And I was too tired to drive anywhere. How could I possibly have the coronavirus? I'd been in my house for three weeks with my teenage daughters and two dogs. An image of the grocery store flashed in my mind . . . I'd worn gloves, but who knew what was on that kale? Or, more accurately, those pints of salted caramel ice cream?

But you couldn't get it from surfaces—I had seen an entire segment on YouTube about that! I moved on to the inevitable next question: "Who got me sick?" Who had I been in contact with? Who had my daughters been in contact with? My mind flashed to a police lineup of acne-faced adolescent boys, smacking gum, knapsacks insolently half slung over their shoulders.

There was an emergency care in the next town that could test me in an hour. So I mustered up enough energy to unearth my insurance card from my tackle box of a wallet and headed out.

It all felt surreal. I had seen enough Hollywood movies like *Pandemic* with Gwyneth Paltrow and Matt Damon and *Contagion* to realize where this was headed as I drove, double masked, into the misty night of uncertainty. I had flashes of Dustin Hoffman in a yellow hazmat suit in the film *Outbreak*, coming toward me with a syringe and a Polaroid of a monkey. I wished I owned a yellow kismet suit.

A quick side note and something that has bothered me for years: When Rene Russo contracted the deadly disease in *Outbreak*, why didn't she have the oozing sores on her face? All the extras who got Ebola were covered in them. She just looked dewy and flushed. Like she'd just had an orgasm, not a deadly virus.

I pulled into the parking lot of the emergency care pop-up. It was sandwiched between a pizza parlor and a Staples. A testing zone carved out of a bankrupt Victoria's Secret store. I had to call the number and let them know I was sitting outside with a mask and rubber gloves and all my paperwork. But before I called, I had to rest my head on the steering wheel. I could feel the virus actively attacking every cell in my body, Pac-Man style . . .

What if I had contracted Covid-19? Up to this point, everything I knew about the disease came from hundreds of hours logged onto cable news and the internet. It was something "out there," in nursing homes, bats, and China, not in my own backyard. Certainly not in my home, where my daughters lived. And Cooper and our obese, incontinent dachshund, Daisy. But then, as one does in times of acute fear, I decided my husband was overreacting, it was allergies, and I was just tired. I was sleeping ten hours a night.

Denial is a broken scale. You know it's broken (you broke it), but you choose to believe you're twenty pounds lighter.

A nurse in a blue hazmat suit and gloves waved me in. I

was whisked onto a seat in a sterile room covered in plastic sheets that had been secured with blue painter's tape. The kind of place where a tidy serial killer would entertain. A doctor entered wearing an even more elaborate suit—this one came with its own shower cap. An outfit designed for surgery on *Grey's Anatomy*, not a temperature read. I have no idea what he looked like, whether he was blond or brunet, but he had a soothing voice.

He took my blood pressure; it appeared to be normal. Huge relief. *I don't have it.*

Then the nose test. A miniature brush, much like the one I used to clean baby bottles when my kids were infants, was inserted up my nose. It burned. Worse than that: it felt like a rod had punctured the outer membrane of my brain. And then a sting. There would be collateral brain damage, for sure.

"What do you think?" I casually asked the doctor. He took my temperature. Fever. He listened to my laborious breathing with a stethoscope. "Oh, I think you definitely have it! Go home and get in bed."

I got into my car and pulled off my masks. Much the way I did with a bra after an evening out—with a combination of anger and relief. How could that doctor say I definitely had it? Wasn't it illegal or against some kind of medical code to make such a casual assertion to a patient?

I pulled out of the grim parking lot. The sky was navy,

and headlights sprinkled up and down the roadway. My breathing became more labored. My mind flashed again to the antismoking ads with the woman without a face. It was getting much worse.

By the time I had passed Kmart, I could feel my body heating up. I clearly had a fever. It was happening.

I felt utterly alone as I white-knuckled the steering wheel. I didn't really know what it meant to have the contagion. I knew it was bad. But I had no idea what the next steps would be. I just hoped Dustin Hoffman would meet me, in his yellow suit, at the staircase with a heating pad and a gallon of matzo ball soup.

Mad
Men
and a
Woman

You never know if your partner will step up to the plate when faced with adversity, natural disasters, or global pandemics. And if you're lucky, you never have to find out. My husband not only stepped up to the plate—he hit it out of the park.

We were engaged after only two months. We didn't have those few trial years to test how we would weather storms. How I, as a young woman, would react if awakened from a lover's dream by a fart. So every hurdle was like jumping off a cliff and praying a billowy cloud would blow by and break our fall. As Steven Wright says, "If at first you don't succeed, then skydiving is definitely not for you."

I was incapacitated. Still in the throes of fever and throbbing joints. Our teenage daughters decided to disappear into an altered state called TikTok as a survival mechanism, and our dogs hibernated into various sofas for the next few months. My husband had to be nurse, mother, father, therapist, breadwinner, cook, laundress, and, in some extreme cases, priest.

His network had sent a van full of tech guys and equipment to our home one wintry day. Our tiny dining room was transformed into a quick and dirty television studio. A pop-up newsroom. A camera, two bright lights, cables taped to the floors and walls . . . All my husband had to do was flip a couple switches and he was live! Imagine the possibilities! I guess it was a good thing I was quarantined in the bedroom. The excitement of a camera that would livestream—well, imagine the possibilities—me in pajama shorts roller-skating to Cardi B, for starters.

My husband would wake up at three a.m. (as he does every day), drink a pitcher of coffee, read the papers, and turn on his little makeshift studio. From the waist up he wore a crisp shirt, jacket, and tie, and from the waist down some boxers and socks. The trickiest part of that live TV experience was making sure the dogs didn't detect a squirrel outside the window and start howling as if they had caught the scent of an escaped convict. If their ears pricked up, he would throw treats on the floor and pray that would distract them until a commercial break.

After the show, he would properly feed the dogs, take out the trash, try to awaken sleeping teenage girls buried beneath eye masks, and bring me a tray of juice and tea. Three times a day he would don a mask and gloves and slide trays of food through the doorway like I was a hostage. Better food, though. I can't imagine hostages ever got roasted scallops with sweet potato puree.

—

But I needed a distraction from my aching body. And the solitary confinement. Each gray day just folded into the next. I felt like Martin Sheen in *Apocalypse Now*, alone in a bare hotel room in Vietnam slowly losing my mind. Sweaty, staring at the bamboo fan flipping round and round. Well, I didn't have a bamboo fan, but you get the idea. Martin Sheen blabbering to himself nonsensical sentences from an unquiet mind. (Okay, I do that even when I don't have Covid.) My head throbbed, and Tylenol PM made me loopy, so I couldn't read. Books were out of the question. And I was too tired to tackle my inbox. (Why is it when you are unwell people bombard you with *How are you?* emails? Chances are—NOT GREAT! And now you have the added burden of having to answer those emails.) I couldn't browse the *Times* or *Drudge Report* because the Covid numbers were too depressing to digest. I needed escapism. Or that twilight stuff they give you before a colonoscopy.

I started on Hulu, then On Demand, then Amazon . . . I'd already devoured all their content by the second month of the pandemic. As I continued scrolling, I stumbled upon the show *Mad Men*, the period drama set in a Manhattan advertising firm in the 1960s and '70s. I had watched the show when it initially came out, but as with so many series, the memory had worn off. And I could barely remember the storylines. Same reason I recently rewatched *Breaking Bad*. And *The Sopranos*. And every season of *Friends*. Don't judge me. Reader, I pushed play.

Mad Men was radical medicine. The combination of fever, delirium, and an award-winning television show that had a stronghold on viewers for seven seasons straight got me through the worst of Covid-19. But not without its own side effects.

I woke up one morning—or it could have been the afternoon; I no longer knew the difference—with heart palpitations and a sense of dread. You see, in my Covid-addled mind, I had been married to Don Draper (played by the irresistible Jon Hamm) for about four years. It was a happy marriage! We made love all the time—and I could wrap my svelte gams around his waist as we stretched out on the psychedelic, sunflower-fabric sofa. We had swinging parties with cheese fondue and gin sizzles. I had double Ds and wore tight jewel-toned dresses that cinched my tiny waist. It was all groovy, except during the parties and sexual romps, nobody was wearing a mask! It caused me tremendous anxiety. The whole agency didn't seem to realize they were at risk of contracting Covid-19. (And probably syphilis.) Clearly, my ample bosom could not tolerate a respiratory infection.

When I woke up I had been smothering my own mouth with a pillow. A rather large face mask, but sometimes the mind and body are not always in sync. Even though I knew, as reality set in, that I was in my bed in 2020, I still couldn't shake the idea that I needed to type an internal office memo reminding the partners to wear masks to the big Coca-Cola pitch.

My husband interrupted my reverie with my favorite snack: fresh orange juice and toast with butter and honey. I never lost my sense of taste and smell. In fact, it was the opposite. My senses were heightened; when I got a whiff of anything being cooked in the kitchen, I would bang my spoon against the wall.

It took a good ten minutes of focusing on the water bug clinging to the ceiling (he had been there for days) before I snapped back to present day. I was not living in the 1960s, where womanizing was rampant, nor was I an alcoholic. I was alone in a dark bedroom with a wooden floor and windows reflecting a gloomy sky and a tumult of rain. I don't drink. But I asked my husband for a martini. "With your toast and honey?" He was right. Instead, I took a Tylenol, placed a cold washcloth on my forehead, and fell back asleep.

The dreams got more and more vivid. And snapping myself out of them began to be more arduous. My sleep pattern was basically a single nap extended around the clock. Sometimes I'd wake up at two a.m. for an hour and then sleep all afternoon. I was on Japan time and London time and LA time. All at the same time.

One afternoon or morning or some shit, I had that surreal sleep experience when your brain flip-flops between a deep level-four and a lighter transcendental meditation nap. In this altered state, the grasp for reality becomes a fool's errand. Nothing makes sense. It's as if both sides of your brain are on mushrooms and there's a tiny clump of lucid cells trapped in the middle screaming, *This isn't happening, #FakeNews!* In this state, I believed I was having a huge fight with my husband, Don Draper. He had cheated on me, once again. And I had had it! It was humiliating. Our marriage had been working! Why would he continually jeopardize it in such a narcissistic and destructive way? I was a big-time fashion model with legs that could crack coconuts and eyelashes that hit my forehead. I was far sexier than any of the secretaries he was taking to hotels that charged by the hour. I even danced for him on his birthday in front of all his friends! In a sequin minidress! To erotic French music! And this was how he repaid me? He was a liar. A predator. A lech. I had hit my limit on what I would take from this very handsome adman who looked stunning in Ray-Bans.

Now, that little cell cluster kept trying to ring the bell alerting me to the fact that none of this was true, but I couldn't pull myself out of the hypnagogic sea. At one point, the alarm on my phone went off. I thrashed around in my bed, sending the phone crashing onto the floor, along with a glass of water. It had to have been an earsplitting crash. But my fevered brain quickly incorporated it into the dream narrative. Don Draper had thrown a crystal decanter of bourbon against the wall because I was threatening to leave him. And the alarm? That was the doorman calling to announce that Roger Sterling was on his way up. I couldn't wait to tell a partner in Don's firm what a heel I had married. Maybe I would even flirt with Roger to get back at Don. After all, two could play at this game, and I was a stunning brunette with pouty lips and not even thirty years old! Wait, I was hotter than Don! I could marry Steve McQueen if I wanted! (At the mention of Steve McQueen, the little clump of cells whispered, *Gurl, this isn't happening and you're in your fifties . . .*)

I have never done hallucinogenics, but I imagine it might feel something like this: stuck between two tectonic plates of uncertainty. The scorned wife narrative dominated. Maybe because my social life consisted of the characters in *Mad Men* and my dog. And fever dreams can do a number on you. Sometimes you have to wait for the fever to break before you open your eyes and take in that realization—you are not the president of the United States or a mermaid or being chased by a dude with a meat mask and a chainsaw.

My fever had not yet subsided; I was twisted up in my sheets like some crazed Martha Graham dancer. When my masked "in real life" husband tapped on the door and slid my dinner tray along the floor—delicious lamb chops and Brussels sprouts with an apple crisp for dessert, with a large glass of ginger ale and ice—I was still caught in 1962.

I grabbed the glass of ginger ale from the tray and threw it on the floor. Tiny shards rained down everywhere. "I WANT A DIVORCE!" I screamed.

My husband quietly turned on the lamp. He gingerly picked up the chunks of glass in his gloved hands and threw them away. With a moist washcloth he wiped sticky soda from the floor and the wall. He handed me a bottle of water and some Tylenol. Took my temperature with the forehead thermometer. Made sure my duvet cover was straightened and fluffed. Picked up some dirty pajamas on the floor.

"I'm going to get you some dulce de leche ice cream," he whispered.

"Thank you," I whispered, and then remembered who and where I was. "BUT DON'T THINK I'M NOT TAKING MY SHARE OF THE STERLING COOPER DRAPER PRYCE AGENCY!"

You Ain't Nothing but a Hound Dog

I had no idea what day it was. Or month, for that matter. The lights were off, so unless I had been flown to Sweden while knocked out by Tylenol PM, it was daytime. I was curled up in the same blue-and-white-striped pajamas, matted hair stuck to the side of my clammy face and one sock still holding on for dear life to my right foot. I had finished all seven seasons of *Mad Men* and had finally returned to the present day. It was a relief to be battling just Covid and not infidelity, alcohol abuse, and corporate takeovers.

I had shifted my focus to local news. It started with being captivated by small stories like "Women from Weight Watchers Shoplift Cupcakes" and grew to getting all my news from the local station. I am a big believer of tuning in to local news wherever you visit. I can tell you all about the tide charts in Camden, Maine. In case you want to go oystering. And especially during a crisis, there is something comforting in knowing how a borough or hamlet is handling its own Covid numbers, food pantries, and daily emergencies. Plus, you can't beat local news banter. When they talk about the weather getting warmer and some male anchor says, "How much do you love sixty-nine!" or "It's Wednesday in Phoenix! A real dry hump day," and they don't pick up on the joke until about ten seconds later and then just freeze . . . THAT'S good TV.

I remember I was watching local Long Island News 12 a few years ago. I was all alone in the house, which was something I had only recently begun praying for. I used to be scared. Then I stopped reading the inside of the *New York Post*.

I had just nestled into what promised to be a perfect evening: the new episode of *The Affair* and a bowl of Corn Pops swimming in whole milk. I was ten minutes early, so I decided to watch local news—if I was lucky, I could catch the "feel-good" animal segment. Nothing better than a baby crocodile stuck in a kiddie pool or a boa constrictor pulling too tight around the weatherman's neck. I always root for the untamed. But that night there was breaking news! And it wasn't about the recycling plant or pit bull puppies being nursed by a cat. A Peeping Tom had been running through the local woods, naked. Well, not completely naked; he wore Nikes. But he had been spotted a few times. They called him a serial nudist. And nobody knew what his agenda was.

I put down my bowl. I thought about getting in the car and driving to a friend's house. But I was terrified to go outside. He was out there, probably hiding in my shrubs. Why was he nude? Should I grab some of my husband's clothes and leave them on the stoop? My heart started to thump, and my hands were shaking. I reached for my cell phone and texted my husband. *Honey, I'm so scared! The news just said there's a naked man running around in the woods!!! He's going to come after me!* There was a long pause. Then he texted back . . . *LOL*. Not the response I was expecting from my knight in shining armor. But then again, I have always been the one more equipped for battle . . .

I never learned what happened to the naked man—he must have gone south in the winter. And *The Affair* episode was the one where Noah and Alison escape to Block Island for the weekend, so I quickly forgot about my fear.

Anyway, back to my Covid afternoon. The local news

story was a good one—a man broke into a bank because he wanted to buy a Hot Pocket. The reporter, who seemed to have confused this incident with Watergate, was pressing the man as she ran beside him, "Was it worth it? Was the Hot Pocket worth it?" "Hell, yeah!!!" the man screamed back. Priceless.

My husband suddenly shouted from the doorway, "Cooper's gone!" What? "Cooper's gone!" Like *Gone Girl* gone? My brain was cooking at 103 degrees, so I needed him to elaborate a little. "What do you mean 'GONE'?" I lifted my head. My husband's response was muffled (he was still talking through the door): "I was taking him on a walk, and he just charged after a deer and disappeared."

I was momentarily speechless. There were so many holes in the story. "Was he on a leash?"

"Yes."

"How did he run off after a deer, then?"

"Well, I had let him off for a minute . . ."

I had a few seconds to decide where my minuscule reserve of energy would be best spent: an argument about my husband's stupidity or a game plan to bring home my emotional support dog. I chose the latter. Debating my husband's intelligence only makes me feel stupid in the end.

"Please, please, honey, go and look for him! I would, but I'M CURRENTLY FIGHTING THE INFECTIOUS

DISEASE THAT IS RAVAGING THE WORLD!" I was met with a dismissive "He'll come back" and the sound of him shuffling down the hall.

Well, now what? I was helpless in my bed, like James Caan in *Misery*. Even if I could put on my sneakers and run down the street, I'd have bat-shit-crazy Kathy Bates chasing me with an axe! Plus, the idea of even brushing my teeth put me back to sleep for a few more hours.

In my feverish nap, I cycled through all the potential Cooper scenarios. He was too sprightly and clever to get hit by a car. But he could have been abducted. Objectively speaking, he was exquisite; he could easily fetch millions on the dark web. He'd definitely gone on a hunt. Or filled up on fawn poop. He always lost track of his surroundings the moment he put his nose to the ground. He could be in Bermuda by now.

"EEEEWWWWWW!!!!!" I heard belted out from downstairs. "GROSSSS!"

Cooper burst through the door into my room with his tongue hanging so low it almost wiped the floor, panting like he had been tied to the back of a bullet train. He was dripping in thick mud, with a smear of what looked like algae across his white chest fur. He was also drenched. Did he swim through a bog? A swamp? Clearly, this was not ocean water but a far more sinister substance.

Curiously, though, Cooper didn't reek. That was the moment I realized I had completely lost my sense of smell. If I'm being completely honest, I think I knew I had lost my sense of smell a couple days earlier, when, after not bathing for days, I took a deep whiff of my armpits and was met with fresh, crystal clear mountain air, when in fact, I must have smelled like a decaying turtle.

I willed myself out of bed for fear Cooper would jump on it and destroy whatever sense of decorum I had left. If I slept in his marshy sludge and muck, I would be in therapy for the rest of my life. I was already this close to starring in an episode of *Hoarders*—empty glasses were piling up on the side table, and my body was constantly exfoliated by all the saltine cracker crumbs in my bed. I had to draw the line somewhere.

As Cooper frolicked about my isolation lair, I could practically see particles of sewage waste gleaming on his fur. Lucky for me, I had a box of gloves at hand, mainly for my husband to clear dishes with. So I snapped on a pair and began chasing the beast around the room. Keep in mind, I had the strength of a pregnant guinea pig at this point, so I had to sit down after one lap around the bed. Finally, between my exhaustion and the fact that he was trapped, we compromised and he allowed me to hoist him into the bathtub. A white porcelain haven that had represented lavender meditations was instantly splattered with the bowels of the earth. And vibrant green globs. I'm going to pretend it was algae or seaweed. But it looked like nuclear waste.

I was on my knees pouring my fancy emollient Living Proof shampoo all over his coat. He would finally get that Jennifer Aniston hair. One hand would scrub his body; the other would steady my weak body as I watched the crud wash down the drain. Bits of garbage, chunks of wild boar hair, a used condom, a baby doll with no arms. Where had my frisky pooch been?

And then I noticed a peculiar thing. Cooper's penis (an appendage I don't ever discuss or concern myself with) was pronounced. Or hadn't retracted. It was not as it should be. This added a whole new layer to the story. Had he been assaulted by a deer? A gang of deer? Sorry . . . a herd?

Finally, Cooper was back to his vibrant white-and-black color. "For hair so healthy, it shines!" Before I put on the finishing touch of a light detangling spray, he had scaled the porcelain wall and jumped out. I didn't have the strength to give chase as I heard him slip and slide down the wooden staircase. And then a cacophony of screams as he, undoubtedly, jumped on the living room sofa, where my daughters were curled up watching *Big Little Lies*, and shook his dripping body all over them.

It took a good twenty-four hours before Cooper's penis retracted into its furry sheath. We'll never know what took place during those hours he went missing. What kind of trauma befell him—alien experimentation, perhaps? All we do know is whenever he sees a deer, he starts shaking uncontrollably.

I thought about the naked man who was running in the woods those years before. And Cooper on his adventure. It confirmed what I have always suspected: I should never leave my house.

Humanity

There are specific rituals that kind and empathetic humans turn to during troubled times. Dropping off a casserole or baked ziti for a grieving person or family—if you're not a cook or baker, dried fruit or an edible bouquet. If someone is having surgery (not elective; it would feel strange sending flowers for a brow lift), a blanket, slippers, or a foot massage will be joyfully received. Perhaps you have a friend getting a divorce—a mug that says I USED TO BE MARRIED, BUT I'M BETTER NOW or a cutting board with their ex's face on it. The point is, the message is clear—*I am thinking of you!* In a "me"-centric, narcissistic culture, I have taken time to carve out a sliver of altruism.

And there are the selfless people who reach out with offerings like childcare, household repairs, and dog walking. Those are the saints.

I like to think I swim somewhere in the pool of concerned

and benevolent people. When I know someone is sick or hurting, I have made a vat or two of homemade beef bourguignon or chocolate chip cookies. In times of death, I've sent white orchids and handwritten cards or offered to run errands and help organize funerals. If someone is new to the neighborhood, I've made laminated books with plumbers' names, take-out menus, and designated dog parks. Now, I'm not tooting my own horn (I've done way better than that—don't get me started on what I DIY for my girlfriends on Valentine's Day), but these fall into the category of what I consider pretty standard acts of kindness. And decency. And they don't stem from a self-serving place; the intent is an authentic expression of goodwill.

I had contracted Covid-19 relatively early on in the scheme of things: if the virus were Godzilla, this was the moment in the movie when it pounded down the street spitting fire, shattering buildings while hundreds of people ran screaming, hiding behind cars and trying to dodge its large reptilian feet.

Everyone was terrified. I had to downplay my illness because my mother had hit level ten on the anxiety meter and there wasn't enough Xanax in Maine to steady her.

It was how people reacted to my prognosis that divided what I considered the high people from the low. It's a juvenile way of looking at it, but I was sick and was very aware about who showed up (metaphorically) and who did not. I think most people use a sieve in difficult times to sift out the people they can count on, who have their back and who would never tell the Nazis that people were hiding under the bed.

I had been bedridden for two weeks; the heavy breathing had turned into a wet cough. My doctor was concerned that it was heading toward pneumonia. She decided on a mega, superpowered antibiotic—the kind that burns through your veins killing everything in its wake. After one dose, I almost turned into the Hulk. The Hulk with a vagina—much scarier.

My husband was shaken by the word "pneumonia." It meant respirator, hospital, and worse. He remained stoic, never for a second showing our children he was crumbling inside. Our doctor instructed him to immediately race out and collect the medicine, just in case they ran out of antibiotics the way they had diapers, thermometers, and toilet paper. He was jolted by the idea that I could get sicker. That I could die.

He sprinted to our local pharmacy in a down coat, face mask, and rubber gloves. He patiently stood in line far behind the person picking up Wellbutrin and Preparation H. But inside, he was Shirley MacLaine screaming through the hospital at the nurses, "GIVE MY DAUGHTER THE SHOT!"

The antibiotics began working almost immediately.

Although I'm sure they eviscerated my pancreas. I was lucky. Extremely lucky. And I never took for granted the fact that I had access to an excellent doctor who could administer the drugs. And that they worked. I thought about the many hundreds of thousands of people whose immune systems could not fight off the virus. The people in the hospitals. The people in the ICUs. The people in the morgues.

A few days later, my phone was blowing up. I had it set to that annoying ping noise to indicate whenever a new email or text arrived. And it started pinging so rapidly—PING PING PING!—I thought a submarine was about to break through the wall. The only other times my phone vibrated with so much activity was when, on our family text feed, there was a furor about who stole the phone charger or what was for dinner. I knew if I even looked at the phone I would end up exchanging food emojis for hours. Ping! Ping! Okay, maybe my husband is texting me about my oxygen level? I fumbled for the phone and a pair of reading glasses. Yes, I'm that person now. If anyone asks me to look at something, I have to flounder around for five minutes looking for gigantic black reading goggles, then pull my hair out of my face, place the glasses on my nose without poking an eye out and bend down to see what the sender is no longer interested in soliciting my opinion on.

It was not about oxygen levels or burgers vs. pizza.

A neighbor had called a local tabloid to slander my husband. Seriously? During a global pandemic? I opened a few links that had been copied and pasted. A pit in my stomach. This woman, a neighbor, someone living in our community, had seen my husband leaving the pharmacy and decided the right way to utilize her energy during a global crisis was to call a tabloid. Her salacious "story" was that I was dying from Covid and he had the audacity to show up at a local gathering place (a pharmacy). Where he could have infected people. Footnote not added: getting an antibiotic so that his wife, who was teetering on full-blown pneumonia, wouldn't have to go to the hospital.

I couldn't and still can't wrap my head around it. He wasn't sneaking out of a motel with an unidentified redhead or stuffing a dead body rolled in a carpet into the trunk of his car. We were all frightened and trying to survive. Where was the empathy? Where was the humanity? Why did this individual choose to train her energy on something that was so small and vindictive?

I was trying to swaddle myself with healing remedies and comfort. I didn't read online tabloid chatter. No matter whose cellulite they proclaimed to expose. There's such a preoccupation with photographing female celebrities and exposing any ounce of fat. And then when a woman over sixty is shot in a bathing suit "she's proving she's still got it." Not that there was much big Hollywood news. Everyone had locked up their Lamborghinis and Porsches. They had bunkered down too. Look, being in the public eye, you are fair game. My husband has been chewed up more than tobacco in every Southern state. But this was different. We were in a pandemic. The enemy was not one another, but this heinous virus that was killing people and destroying lives. Most of our community was supporting food banks and helping frontline workers. People were risking their own lives to come to the aid of others. We were looking for safe havens for people suffering from physical abuse or being chased by ICE and for seniors unable to get food and water for themselves. Our minds automatically leaned into a collective sense of duty. And that's what you want when the nation is on fire, a wave of benevolence. We were ALL IN THIS TOGETHER! Or so I thought . . .

I had never met this woman. Still haven't. So there was no revenge scenario. I hadn't keyed her car, nor had my husband dumped her sister in college. I even went on her social media accounts to get a sense of the person who'd called the tabloids on my husband. We shared no groups, connections, or likes. I searched for any thread that would help me make sense of it. I could have understood it if it was a matter of strained circumstances, someone really struggling during a difficult time, but there was no sign of that. In fact, she was out playing golf during most of Covid.

What was the endgame? Was she trying to fill some emotional void? I imagined a woman who wasn't listened to, at home or at her job. Perhaps being overlooked was the undercurrent of her life. And she had grabbed a moment. A moment to be witnessed.

I thought about the *New York Times* writer Arthur Brooks, who said, "America is being ripped apart by bitterness and contempt, fomented by public bullies and self-interested leaders—but we can fight back to reunite the nation around principles of respect, kindness, and dignity." Perhaps we *had* become a nation of contempt. And that notion made me sicker than any virus battling my immune system.

We had new neighbors who had moved in a few months earlier. Back when the idea of a plague was the provenance of horror films and apocalyptic television shows. We hadn't met. Not even a moment when cars pass and there's a quick wave. In warmer months, I would hear murmurs through the bushes or the sound of a lawn mower. I concluded from some bumper stickers that our politics were different. But that was all the data I had.

My husband entered my room, kitted out like a surgeon about to scrub in. He handed me an envelope that had been left in our mailbox. Inside was a card that read, *We hear you are sick. We are so sorry. Please let us know if we can help in any way. If you need groceries or anything. Feel better soon . . . Your neighbors.*

One pandemic. Two neighbors.

I never thought I would quote a fable in any of my books.

But I do this to reinforce my story because it is a teachable tale and it did rattle my optimistic outlook. Plus, if I use one of Aesop's fables, my mother will definitely read this.

A Lion used to prowl about a field in which Four Oxen used to dwell. Many a time he tried to attack them; but whenever he came near they turned their tails to one another, so that whichever way he approached them he was met by the horns of one of them. At last, however, they fell a-quarrelling among themselves, and each went off to pasture alone in a separate corner of the field. Then the Lion attacked them one by one and soon made an end of all four. United we stand, divided we fall.

All for
Pizza

Phase three—New York state had opened up a bit more. Andrew Cuomo had become the pinup boy for global pandemics, with women declaring their love for him on memes and social media. (Ironically, this was less than a year before his resignation due to a barrage of sexual harassment allegations.) Stores were open with a limited number of customers as long as they masked up and showered in the jug of hand sanitizer placed on a rickety stool in front. A smattering of restaurants opened, but only outdoors: futuristic-looking plastic bubbles were popping up throughout Manhattan filled with makeshift tables and plastic chairs, ambience created by a few dying houseplants and Christmas lights. People were cautiously dipping their toes into social waters.

I was invited to a socially distant, mask required, outdoor pizza dinner for under twenty people. At least that's what the invite said. It had been months. My social circle consisted of my husband and two daughters, along with Cooper (and his stench) and Daisy, the obese dachshund who refused to poop outside. The lines were starting to blur as to who was human. I needed to have conversations with people other than my news anchor husband, who delivered daily somber updates, and teenagers who emerged from their rooms only for a PowerBar or to inform me they needed toilet paper. I wanted to believe "things were getting back to normal." And talk to other human beings about their experiences during this time instead of viewing the curated versions on Snapchat. To make real eye contact. To catch a scent of perfume. To learn to read gestures and other social cues again. Okay, truth. I couldn't bear making another dinner. I was caught in a meal prep version of *Groundhog Day*.

Now, we were in a pandemic! The numbers were still worrisome, the decision to go to a small gathering still fraught. But in my mind, venturing out (taking all the precautions in transit, of course) for a few slices of sausage, jalapeño, and red pepper pizza seemed relatively safe and, even more important, a mental health life raft. Again, I don't drink alcohol, smoke weed, or pop Xanax (okay, twice a year, max), so I view dough and cheese as my comparatively healthy vice. Or I did until my recent cholesterol test caused my doctor to gasp and shout, "Holy shit!" then hug me and place me on the highest possible dose of Lipitor. But at the time, a slice of pizza felt like it would stave off a couple of dark days under the down comforter.

The concept of departing from the quarantine uniform of pajama top and sweatpants seemed completely alien. And unnecessary. But it was one of the first social outings in a long time, and it's only courteous as a guest to adhere to the social norms of presentation. And hygiene. So I showered. It's amazing what a little toothpaste and a razor can do! And I unwrapped a bottle of room spray from last Christmas that smelled like a burning fir tree. So I smelled nice. Oh, who gives a shit, we were in a pandemic. I opted for black dress pants and a gray linen sweater. No makeup, of course—let's not get crazy. I wasn't meeting the Queen of England or accepting the Nobel Peace Prize.

I arrived wearing a floral-print mask. I'd been saving it for a special occasion. It was too fancy to be worn to the IGA bottle drop or the dump. My last gesture of femininity made its debut on a manicured lawn for twenty sets of eyes to behold, before it would be crumpled and lost in the side pocket of our car.

When I arrived, the sparse mingling had already commenced. Masked faces holding glasses of cocktails awkwardly trying to remember how to stand and make small talk. As opposed to slovenly lying on the sofa grasping a bottle by its neck. It was like *Night of the Living Dead* as people fumbled around antiquated greeting rituals.

The pandemic had erased the art of chitchat. It was an unprecedented time, and you couldn't ignore the fact that we were all frightened and uneasy about the future. Of the world. I'm sure during the Spanish Flu of 1918, people didn't stand around discussing the hardships of not being able to get a decent haircut. I can talk about the weather for about twenty seconds, but only if it's snowing in July.

I had escaped my lair like some kind of night-stalking woodland creature and wanted to make the most of my time as a communal animal in the daylight. I shuffled over to a friend who happens to be a television journalist. He obviously needed a slice of sausage, jalapeño, and red pepper pizza too. It was comforting to see him truly live and not cable streaming live.

Jared was in his off-camera attire: Bermuda shorts, a T-shirt, and some sort of man sandal. Not so much Herodian Kingdom Birkenstock as dapper globe-trotting espadrille? He was sipping on some cocktail that looked tangy orange and exotic, enticing enough to seduce a toddler into drinking. Jared clearly wanted a break from the onslaught of disheartening news. I was looking for a bit of substance. Anything with gravitas. Or a dirty joke. You know, banter that expands the mind. I joined him and a skeletal Lee Radziwill–looking woman in an ornate, embroidered kaftan. "I adore cherrystones if they're not too big." Lady Kaftan chuckled. Before Jared responded with some inane comment about cockles or steamers, I butted in. "This is such a fucking awful time!" Lady Kaftan looked at me like I had just peed on her foot. Jared gave me a grateful look of recognition. "It's really awful. I'm getting death threats." Well, that was quite enough for Lady Kaftan. She was not at a mini soiree with freshly painted nails and a full clutch of gossip to be wrestled down into the muck and mire of current events. She sprinted over to a man talking about sports. It must have been her husband, because their outfits were color-coordinated.

Just as we were broaching that old cocktail-party conversation chestnut—Can democracy be saved?—the hostess announced that it was time to sit down. She wore a dress that fit like a condom. Same color too—I guess you would call it exposed cream? And very high heels. If I wore those heels I would look like a baby goat learning to walk. Her hair was blown dry, and her makeup was applied with professional precision. Again, this was for pizza. In a pandemic. (Later that night, I had an idea. What if I rented an old ice cream truck and drove around from neighborhood to neighborhood offering bikini waxes, highlights, and Botox. I would have the same melodic chimes as the ice cream truck and would cruise up and down the streets of all the suburbs on the East Coast. Can you see it? Women in heels running after the truck like rabid children chasing Good Humor Chocolate Éclair bars . . .)

There was a long outdoor table with flowers and plastic utensils. One table. Seated. And not six feet apart. More like six inches. I hesitantly sat down; it felt a little like Covid roulette. But I was pleasantly distracted by my seatmate, one of my favorite people, Leonard, a comedy writer with a filthy mind and an arsenal of tasteless jokes. I am drawn to people who can carry on a nonverbal conversation using only campy faces and obscene gestures. We shared a whole sausage pizza drenched in hot honey. Our mouths were splattered with tomato sauce as I gulped down six club sodas and he matched me with straight tequila. It was a mental release to laugh. For me, a shared guffaw is the most gratifying human connection. Before I was married, I would have been elated to lie in bed with a man and laugh instead of having sex. Sometimes the two went hand in hand.

I gazed down the table at Jared. He was seated next to an architect who had long, thick salt-and-pepper hair. Not the kind you want to run your fingers through, the kind you want to cut. I could tell by the banal hand gestures that the conversation was one step above cherrystone clams.

Across from me was a striking, rather reserved man. Leonard had wandered off to the bathroom (or to get more tequila), so I decided to engage. After all, this might be the last pizza party for a long time. After tonight, I would go back to talking to the people on the TV as if they were in the room. I've never met Rachel Maddow, but we are best friends.

Early on in the conversation with my new tablemate, I assumed it would involve a lot of heavy verbal lifting on my part, mostly because he was soft-spoken. He then divulged that he was a sex therapist. For the LGBTQ community. An unexpected gift. I had so many questions. I could have done a three-hour podcast with him. We discussed gender identity, internalized homophobia, monogamy . . . I turned back to my funny comedy friend Leonard, who was trying to scheme how to steal a stack of pizzas and hide them in the back of his car. Possibly resell them. We were on our second (okay, maybe fourth) sausage pie. A few seats down, Lady Kaftan was picking vegetables off the top of a pizza, and then, like a surgeon, slicing off the layer of cheese. She finally resorted to using her fingernails. She was left with soggy tomato bread. Kind of defeats the purpose of pizza.

"Is this gluten-free crust?" she asked no one in particular.

I prayed our paths would never cross again.

I scoured the party. People drinking too much, eating too much, avoiding too much and desperately trying to appear poised in an extremely surreal moment in our lives. But there was an undertow of fear. And it was palpable. Human beings aren't good with the unknown. There's no control in that. Which is why we spend billions to go to space and build mausoleums for the afterlife.

The hostess's son casually came out of the house and started kicking a soccer ball around the backyard. Probably taking a break from his tenth hour of playing Minecraft.

"I feel so bad for him," the hostess said. "Not seeing any of his friends. We only let him see his cousin. He hasn't smiled in months." I thought about the mental health crisis our country was steeped in, particularly our children. And shoved a very large spoonful of whipped cream into my mouth.

Leonard stood up from the table.

"Hey kid!" he yelled to the boy. "Over here!"

The kid passed him the ball. And soon the two were on the lawn kicking it back and forth. As I finished the bowl of whipped cream, I wondered: when was the last time my daughters were outside?

Then Jared stood up and sauntered over to Leonard, who passed him the ball. Jared kicked it back. Soon the architect placed down his napkin and walked out on the grass. I prayed he wouldn't gather his long hair into a man bun.

"Are you guys seriously going to play soccer?" the hostess yelled. If her shoes were any indication, this was not what she had planned.

Leonard summoned me. I waved him off. "I'm good!"

"Oh come on, work off some of that pizza!" All 16,000

calories, I thought? And reluctantly moseyed over to their little man clan. When the soccer ball glided over to me, I gave it a soft kick.

An hour later, goals had been set up on either end of the yard, white lawn chairs subbing in for posts. The whole table had joined what became a heated match (yes, even Lady Kaftan). All in bare feet. Someone would occasionally run off to get a swig of water. There were screams and cheers and hugs. Lady Kaftan flew down the yard using one hand to hold up her robe as she walloped the ball into the goal. The hostess had shed her suede heels; her dress had dirt smeared across the back from a fall outside the foul line.

"I'm going to get you, you son of a bitch," she yelled at Leonard as she chased him, bony knees flashing.

"Is there any more pizza?" he screamed back.

"Jesus, Leonard, I saw you put four pies in your car!"

It was a sea of grass-stained pants and dirty hems. Even the hostess's son had eventually become a bystander as the game evolved into a soccer fight club. Everyone in their most primal form, sprinting, grabbing, rolling, tagging, and laughing. The exterior armor had disappeared, along with all traces of lipstick. Human beings, in their raw state, trying to purge the fears of the previous months.

As dusk settled in people gathered for goodbyes. All of us holding our shoes. Our collective dread left on the field.

I slept well that evening. Yes, because my sloth-like body

hadn't hit such a high heart rate in a while, but also because my mind felt more at rest.

Leonard called a few days later. He had too much tequila that night and although he was an excellent forward and scored a goal for our team, he had forgotten all about the pizzas he'd stashed in the back seat of his car.

The Island

I spent more time with my husband and daughters during the height of the pandemic than I have with any other group of people in my life, and that includes my siblings, my tent mates at Camp Treetops, and my conjoined twin. Well, if I had one. I'm #Grateful, don't get me wrong, but I can't help but wonder what the long-term ramifications will be on two teenage girls who were locked down with their parents for such an excruciatingly long period of time. Teenagers are not meant to spend that amount of condensed time with their creators, let alone themselves. They should be kissing and getting their hearts broken, battling bullies and getting caught throwing parties when the parents are away for the weekend. But my kids knew that a rager was not in the future for a very long time. Because we weren't going anywhere for a very long time. Not that I wanted them out in the woods dropping molly and giving hand jobs, but they were starting to live too chaste a life in our de facto monastery.

It's kind of a miracle when you consider that we all made it through intact. Well, with the exception of the *Freaky Friday* episode where my husband and I turned into teenagers.

It began the first day I had finished my three-week Covid quarantine and descended the stairs. Like a monk leaving the monastery after a long monastic practice.

Or more accurately, like a prisoner emerging from solitary confinement to discover that all hell had broken loose in the prison yard. I wasn't prepared for the state of our home. And it wasn't just dishes stacked in the sink, clothes strewn all over the floor, and bathroom trash bins overflowing. No. It was on par with a frat house after March Madness. I'm talking about cereal bowls with the milk hardened like glue on the sides and spoons standing upright. Under the sofa. Empty bags of chips left on the mantel. Dog urine sprayed in a paisley motif across the carpet. It was *Animal House*. Literally and figuratively. As of that moment I wanted to put my family on double secret probation.

The next day, I had a vacuum hose around my neck and a bucket of Windex and Soft Scrub hanging off my wrist. I was going to scour the degradation and polish the layers of neglect. But thirty minutes into a rigorous session, I collapsed on the couch. Sure, remnants of Covid. But more a sense of *Who gives a shit?* Just exactly who or what was I cleaning for? I was flitting around like Emma Thompson in *Remains of the Day*. As if Meghan and Harry were coming over for vichyssoise and tomato aspic. It occurred to me that during a pandemic, one could be a little lax when it came to domestic perfection. So I yanked the vacuum cord out of the wall and settled in for a pint of mint Oreo cookie ice cream. That's called breakfast in pandemic-speak. And then I left the empty, dripping container on the coffee table next to a dried piece of spaghetti.

Family dinner used to be twenty minutes. At most. Because of homework and extracurricular academic commitments, baked ziti was shoveled in, dishes thrown in the sink followed by the sound of my girls' doors closing in unison. My husband would go walk the dogs, and I would be alone in the kitchen cleaning up. That is our contract. The girls clear the table. George walks the dogs, and I shine the kitchen. And by the time I am finished, you could eat off my floor.

That was before the plague hit.

Dinners during lockdown lasted between forty-five minutes and two hours. Suddenly, there was no lacrosse, no homework, no bedtime, and a very foggy future. And food became the main source of hope and optimism. Our family group chat was filled with screenshots from Instagram or some random person's blog about baking bread as the means to preserving our sanity. At breakfast, we discussed what we would have for dinner. Even though we dreamt big, it was based on what we had in the fridge—we ventured out as little as possible, and the market required gloves, a mask, bags, hand sanitizer, and a strong sense of physical boundaries. Chicken tacos became the thing that got us through many months. Our freezer looked like it belonged to a poultry serial killer.

During dinner, we had rabid discussions about equality and social injustice. We debated the death penalty, the environmental crisis, and the lack of medical research for women. And as the parental units we ignited debates and, sometimes in a very didactic tone, educated them on historic context.

And then, sometime in late spring, it all changed. We changed. Not in the sense of an evolution. Actually, the opposite: my husband and I started Benjamin Buttoning into the same emotional maturity as our teenage daughters. I fell into a vernacular that mirrored my Gen Z offspring's, starting most of my sentences with *What the fuck?*s and *sucks to suck*s. And I allowed my youngest to use the same language and, at times, even worse. Family dinners in which we handed down parental wisdom were a thing of the past; we no longer prefaced our opinions with "You know, when I was a young person . . ." We were four teenagers shooting the shit about how disgusting the popular alcoholic seltzer White Claw was. And why Black Cherry White Claw provokes vomiting. We had discussions about QAnon and conspiracy theories. I'd had no idea Katy Perry is really Jon-Benét Ramsey! We forgot to put our napkins in our laps. Hell, we forgot napkins, period. We threw scraps right at Cooper, who caught them like a shark. We blared Taylor Swift. A few times we even brought our phones to the table— a rule that had been etched in stone. And much like with the vacuum, I gave up and just let things get dirty.

At some point during Covid, we ran out of things to watch on TV. Netflix? Done. Amazon? Done. Hulu? Done. National Geographic? Done. And then one day our youngest discovered *Love Island Australia*. The show features a group of single contestants, known as "islanders," who live together in a villa that is isolated from the outside world, in an attempt to find love. The islanders are continuously monitored during their stay in the house by live television cameras as well as personal audio microphones. Throughout the series, the contestants "couple up" to avoid being dumped from the villa. At various points in the series, Australians vote for their favorite islanders; as old islanders are dumped, new islanders enter the villa. A revolving door of barely dressed singles. Not exactly a Ken Burns film or *My Octopus Teacher*. A raunchy show about super-toned, spray-tanned people hooking up.

When my daughter first invited me to join her in

exploring this nude frontier, I rolled my eyes. I've never watched *The Bachelor* or any insta-couple reality shows. Only because it makes me too anxious. Oh, and it's completely misogynistic. But little by little, I got sucked in. The way a person rubbernecks on a highway. I would watch a scene here or there. Sometimes it was just a couple having sex in a room with six other couples surrounding them. Gross. And I would scream. It advanced to the point where I would watch a scene, scream, and then actually pull up a chair. Then, soon enough, it evolved into a family ritual. *Love Island* time meant claiming your chair in the living room with a throw, a bowl of ice cream, and elated anticipation. As much as I cursed at the screen about indecent shorts and sex based on committee (I sounded like Anita Bryant or some Christian evangelist's wife), we kept watching season after season. Until we knew all their names, who they had hooked up with, and every catchphrase from the show. If you watch *Love Island*, you will understand why we walked around our house yelling, "I got a text!"

You may or may not be familiar with Cameo, the app that allows you to request custom videos for a few hundred bucks from celebrities like Chuck Norris, Bethenny Frankel, or Blac Chyna. Imagine my youngest daughter's surprise when we bought a cameo from a cast member on *Love Island*! A blond woman in a thong bikini wishing my girl a happy birthday (or *hoppy bathday, mate*)! We used to give her aspirational books or complicated craft kits for her birthday. But not during quarantine! We gave her the once-in-a-lifetime gift of an iPhone video of a woman in a bikini who was voted off an island for not being fuckable enough.

One night we were watching some inappropriate movie that six months before we would not have even allowed our fourteen-year-old to see the trailer for, and one of the characters in the film mentioned a blow job. I froze, then tried to slyly turn around and catch a glimpse of her expression. "I know what that is, Mom!" I slumped into my chair, my hand across my mouth. I wanted to put her back in the BabyBjörn. But it was too late. There were no secrets anymore, no nuance. We were just a crew of teenagers draped around the furniture watching R-rated films. Whatevs.

Little by little, all the old rules evaporated. Bedtimes were up to the individual, because who cares when you don't have something definitive to wake up for? Sleep all day, look at memes all night. Nothing matters. If you went to the kitchen in the middle of the night for raw frozen cookie dough, undoubtedly, you would run into one of us eating cold spaghetti.

My daughters and I started rotating the same outfit. Our clothes became communal. A few sets of cozy fleece pajama pants and sweatshirts. We walked around like gigantic babies in onesies. You could only tell I was the parent because of the wrinkles and age spots.

All of this came to a head one March night. My youngest decided we should have a theme dinner. Just like any fraternity or stunted-growth-adult birthday party—it's as if we were all competing for who would go insane first. And the theme of the soiree? *Love Island Australia*. Even my husband participated. He wore his bathing trunks. I wore a bikini (I was so pale my skin was light blue) and heels. My daughters wore bikinis, heels, and enough eye shadow to paint a house. And there the four of us stood in our kitchen. Like a group of carnies that had been on the road way too long. Or a Diane Arbus photo that never sold.

We gobbled our chicken tacos. Nothing like chowing down on melted cheese in a bikini to give yourself a little ego boost. After we had fully stuffed ourselves and the lipstick had faded, the girls decamped to their rooms, phones in hand. Cooper jumped up onto the table and started eating remnants off the plates. We had become completely unglued. No sense of decorum. Our dignity being lapped up like the bits of tortilla going into our dog's mouth. I froze, my bloated belly quivering over my bikini bottoms. And then I lost it.

I stomped my heels. Standing there pulling the bikini ruffle out of my butt crack, I was hardly the image of parental authority, but I had outrage on my side. "Hey! This has gotten completely out of hand!" I recall throwing a spoon at the sink. "You two are doing the dishes!" My eldest daughter came back into the kitchen. "Why are you yelling?" I stomped a heel again. "I'm not cleaning up! You hear me? I am not doing the dishes again!" My daughter looked at me calmly. "Fine. You don't have to scream. Just get out of here. Go to your room!"

My husband and I slunk off to our bedroom, whispering to each other as we closed the door and tried to process what had just happened. "So, do we just stay here until they say we can come out?"

"I guess."

"Well, what are we supposed to do now?"

"I don't know."

"Want to watch *Love Island UK*?"

"Fuck yeah!"

Rake
It Out

What to do in a lockdown? It's not a vacation. It's not a temporary leave. It's an unknown period of fear and death with no predetermined outcome or end point. There's no manual of coping skills except to survive. And, hopefully, help your fellow humans to survive as well.

So we quarantine. And spray down food, counters, surfaces, and ourselves. We support local charities, food pantries, elderly who need supplies. We have the news on around the clock, searching for meaning and any progress toward a vaccine. We wait. We pray. We devour too much butter.

And then there's the mental component. Our brains go on automatic pilot. We are told to do these things; we do them. We wear masks, we social distance, we don't have huge key parties with the neighbors. But what to do when we lie down at night and are confronted with the existential threat of our state of being, our mortality? I had huge bouts of insomnia. And it wasn't due to menopause, spicy food, or melatonin immunity. I simply could not quiet my mind. There was no relying on the government, my horoscope, or a higher power to assure me that all would be well. We were in free fall. The creative right and the analytic left sides of my brain agreed to join forces and fixate on apocalyptic scenarios that involved tidal waves, the gestapo, and zombies. Was it the end of the world and we didn't realize it? It started with dinosaurs and ends with the Kardashians and Bitcoin? Deep down, I had always known the human race would not be able to sustain itself if it didn't pay attention to things like global warming, biological warfare, tribalism, social media, and the people who go barefoot on airplanes.

I tried meditation, breathing exercises. Counting backward. All the cognitive tools. But every mental image that started with me floating in the sea ended with a shark attack. Whenever I tried to meditate on family gatherings in the past, I would end up alone amongst carnage of broken-down cars and empty buildings. Even watching *Peppa Pig*, a cartoon anthropomorphic sow, couldn't calm my amygdala (the part of your brain that governs your survival instincts), so instead, I would turn the TV off before she became bacon.

I'm not a Grateful Dead head. Dude, I love the music. I miss Jerry. But I'm not the type to surrender to a cloud of bong smoke "rolling in the bushes down by the riverside." Yet I thought about getting high—I was at the point where psychoactive plants felt like the only possible solution. After all, cannabis was the new plastics. I could procure edibles more easily than toilet paper. Ultimately, the fear that I would go on a bad trip that would exacerbate the (already off-the-charts) angst prevailed, however. To quote the immortal Charlie Brown, "even my anxieties had anxieties."

At the beginning, I baked, like everyone else. To be fair, I was way ahead of the curve on this one: I have always loved to bake. The ritual. The pleasure of seeing the excitement on my kids' faces when it's something chocolate and not beets. The comfort of the smell wafting from the kitchen. They say the secret to selling a house is to bake cookies right before a showing. But the endless parade of cookies, crumbles, and cakes lost its luster after a few weeks. And the sweets were no longer being devoured. Even the food pantries wouldn't accept unsolicited brownies.

Crafts were never my thing; I just never fully engaged in knitting, crocheting, or bejeweling jeans. I tried painting rocks, which was my go-to when the girls were little. But it felt empty painting a rock when there was no one to admire my handiwork. I fully understand why seniors get together and play Jenga and bridge. Someday (soon) I'm going to assemble a coffee klatch group, and we are going to paint rocks. So there's something to look forward to.

In the early weeks, I cleaned out the basement. Anything to distract from the monsoon of uncertainty gathering in the distance. I categorized photos. I threw out miscellaneous crap I'd thought was integral at the time, like a boarding pass for the Delta shuttle to DC from 1998. I hit the jackpot one rainy afternoon when I found a duct-taped box, belonging to my husband, which contained old love letters. Well, "love letters" is an exaggeration; they were correspondences. But a delicious way to spend the afternoon. The letters also triggered a tinge of jealousy, which resulted in a very sultry evening. (I have always found jealousy and possessiveness to be a better aphrodisiac than oysters and champagne.) As the weeks went on, I alphabetized books, creating huge mounds of paperbacks to donate to the local library. Like the copy of *The Scarlet Letter* from high school in which I'd highlighted all the wrong things. And an antiquated yacht club cookbook with recipes like cod dip (which is fish and a ton of mayo).

I rearranged the pantry. That was out of necessity. Everyone deals with stress differently. Cooper's way is to break into the pantry late at night and help himself. Sometimes it's a box of spaghetti. Or a bag of chocolate chips, dried seaweed crackers, and once some instant coffee. Each morning brings evidence of his nightly carnage. Sometimes a chewed plastic container, a few scattered rigatonis, or just a stinking pile of diarrhea.

I FaceTimed girlfriends who were also searching for activities to stave off the dark cloud. They were tackling the same arduous tasks, except with label makers, which made me very envious. But these small domestic chores offered a steady path and the will to keep going. Years ago, when I was fighting my way through a depression, my mother offered me an English muffin with sliced tomatoes. That was how she dealt with fear, by using tools that had been handed down from generation to generation in her family. It made her feel like she was doing something to help me, but it was really a mechanism to help her. As much as I love a toasted crumpet, shock therapy would have been a better choice.

When the months grew warmer, I ventured outside for walks or to hit tennis balls. No, there was no access to tennis courts. I should clarify, I hit muddy tennis balls with a broken yard-sale tennis racket around the backyard while Cooper chased them and chewed them into rubbery bits. Not quite Wimbledon. But you should see Cooper chase tennis balls after a night of feasting on a bag of instant coffee—talk about doping!

I remembered I had gone clamming the summer before (pre-Covid) with my friend Brooke. It had struck us as an adventurous thing to do. So we bought some clam rakes and went into the bay and started raking. We should have Googled "clamming for dummies." We would have learned to go at low tide, not high. As it was, we were basically hoeing the bottom of the bay. We came home with nothing but sore backs and some hilarious photos of our asses sticking up in marsh grass. But I was hooked. Like diving for shells, there is a treasure-hunt element to the endeavor that I find irresistible. You lose yourself and all sense of time when you're out in nature foraging for food.

So, like most people desperate for batteries, books, and pimple cream, I logged on to Amazon yet again. Thanks to my two teenage girls' shopping habits during the pandemic, Jeff Bezos can now buy the rest of the Northern Hemisphere. I ordered a full-body wader jumpsuit with attached rubber Wellies and a new clam rake. (The other one broke when I used it to secure a hole in our fence with a cement block. We have an obese dachshund who's the Houdini of sausage dogs. I've used crates, a plastic tray, a Christmas tree stand, and bits of chicken wire to plug holes she has dug underneath that fence. She always finds a new place to dig her little claws in and squeeze her fat loaf of a body through. But she always comes back for dinner.)

Finally, the day came when my Amazon package of gear was hoisted over the fence, landing with a thud that was followed by the sound of barking dogs. That's how we knew we'd gotten a package—we'd hear a thump of something hitting the driveway or lamppost or dog.

This time I did my research and knew to hit the mucky

inlet at low tide, which was three o'clock in the afternoon in June. Clams depend on the turbidity of the water.

So off I drove, with a long wooden clam rake sticking out of the back of my car. Windows down, "Sugar Magnolia" blaring.

When I got to the secluded landing, there was nothing surrounding me but the bay and a titanium-colored sky. Not a person, boat, snowy egret, or screeching seagull. It was the first time during the pandemic that I could venture out without worrying about human contact or enclosed spaces. It was eerily still and quiet. It felt like either the end of the world or the beginning. I left my flip-flops in the sand and hoisted up my rubber outfit. I forgot sunscreen. But skin cancer was low on the list of my current fears. I put on my *Gilligan's Island* hat, grabbed my rake, and started schlepping through the glop.

At low tide you don't have to bother with straining rocks and clams through the murky water. You can just rake the moist surface sand and see the hint of bivalve molluscs. Beautiful blue round jewels of the sea. Your heart beats hard when you unearth your first one. I think that's how the pioneers felt during the gold rush. For me, it's as if I just burglarized Harry Winston and pulled a ten-carat diamond out of the black velvet pouch. I would hold the clam up to the sun and admire it, checking its girth and calcareous valves.

I tucked the first clam in the pocket of my jumpsuit. But after I had amassed a handful, I threw them in the plastic grocery bag that was fastened to my belt. I pulled one gorgeous northern quahog after another until my bag was weighing down my right side. There's an addictive quality, like playing the slots in Vegas: "One more and then I'm done," I would repeat over and over to myself. Until I was so weighted down I trudged out of the bay like a waterlogged Santa Claus.

I have to warn you—if you're someone who likes a nice manicure, shapely tips and a light pink gloss, this activity is not for you. After clamming, my hands look like they just served on an oil rig. You gotta scrub that dirt and grime from under your nails with the same scour brush you use on the clams. And your hands get calloused from the rake. You need a special salve to help the cracked skin and chapped palms I share with the cast of *Deadliest Catch*.

The clams were scrubbed and soaked in ice water. And from there I made linguine with clams, baked clams, grilled spicy clams, clams casino, and garlic bread clams. If I knew how to TikTok, I'd have billions of hits.

Just when my husband thought, *Dear Lord, make these endless bowls of crustacean in the fridge stop*, I decided to build a vegetable garden. If I built it, they would come. Gathering the main course is one thing, but what about the side dishes? I would grow, gather, and cook all our meals! If I could only find a butter churn and a covered wagon!

An essential ingredient of a thriving garden is direct sunlight. Who knew? Mine was in the shade all afternoon. It was really a garden box. About eight by ten feet with too much sod and not enough fish fecal matter. But it produced many cucumbers and tomatoes! The squash strangled the beets, and the zucchini wilted. The basil took over half the garden, battling the mint for domination. But all in all, I was able to produce about six salads. With the money I spent on the wood, soil, seeds, plants, plant grower, shovels, and floral gloves, I could have bought eight Olive Gardens. But it was a noble attempt. And it kept that cloud of worry at bay.

What I found through all my pioneer woman pursuits was an ability, in its most pure form, to distract myself and retain a sense of optimism. And also avoid popping Xanax. My coping tools were real tools: rakes, hoes, shears, and buckets. With these in my life, I was finally able to sleep. Clamming is not just satisfying, it's physically exhausting. Imagine if Jane Fonda had embraced fishery instead of aerobics in the 1980s.

I had found nirvana in the surf and turf. I was renewed, and a little obsessed. I started reading local fishing blogs. There's an annual biggest clam contest. Last year's winner had a clam that weighed over two pounds! I have plotted out, via maps, graphs, and word of mouth, exactly where the big fellas dwell. Next summer I plan on bringing home the gold. Or a DIY clam statue. And a vat of chowder.

One afternoon a clam digger described a police vehicle cruising the shores asking to see shellfish licenses and writing up huge fines.

SHELLFISH LICENSE?

What if I were arrested? Prisons are in crisis with Covid! How many years do you get for shellfishing without a license? I don't remember any of the women from *Orange Is the New Black* in the big house for hauling scallops! I considered the adrenaline rush of being a fugitive clammer. The FBI searching for me from one body of water to another. From the Florida Keys to Nova Scotia.

I am now a proud holder of a shellfish digger permit. It's a real badge of honor. It's like I'm the mayor of clam town.

It Could Happen to Me

After months in lockdown, I realized I was never going to achieve any of my aspirational goals. No, not weight loss. The ones I set at the beginning of quarantine. The ones about taking advantage of the time and rereading Chaucer, learning Mandarin, and practicing meditation. I would glare at the blank two-by-four-foot canvas I'd bought, the new paintbrushes still upright in a mason jar. I tried to write but ended up Googling "at-home remedies to tighten your neck flesh." Something happens to one's creative libido when forced into a cage of infinite time. And you're left in a discontented and unfulfilled state, except when melting marshmallows with a fork over the stove.

But that's an entirely different proposition: that's pure survival.

There's a saying, "If you want something done, ask a busy person," which has always resonated with me. If I have a blank calendar one day, the idea of gassing up the car is overwhelming. But if I have a packed day of meetings, dentist appointment, school conference, and scripts due, I can not only gas up my car, but gas up the state of New York. I can accomplish Herculean things if I'm going at high speed. So in the pandemic, when everything screeched to a halt, so did I.

At the beginning of Covid-19, I was spinning. I drove over the speed limit to Costco to load up on chicken nuggets and bottled water. I worked with other women in my community on a fund to help underserved families. I made sure my aging parents were secure and had supplies. I had a million checklists. And frozen logs of cookie dough. Survival. Survival. Survival.

But six months in, the country had plateaued into a sedentary state, and I found making toast debilitating. I wasn't alone. All those cheerful Instagram posts of bread—rye bread, sourdough bread, braided bread—testaments to the illusion that we were all not just surviving but flourishing and thriving in a difficult time: vanished. We were in a universal creative slump. The virus had stamped out the will to create. Or even fake it.

I lay on the sofa, surfing the web, channels, Twitter. I would flip through the *New York Times*, perusing the real estate section. The obituaries. I also became obsessed with the Science section on Mondays. Ask me anything about sea slugs and flesh-eating ulcers.

And then I saw it. Well, I saw her name. Annabelle Gurwitch. I had known her years and years ago. I'm not giving the exact year on the chance Annabelle lies about her age. She is an actress. As am I. But I was outed years ago and can no longer turn thirty-six every year. At some point I am going to need to turn thirty-seven. Anyway, Anabelle is a striking redhead with chutzpah. Without sounding like a blurb on the back cover of one of her books, she is sharp-eyed, un-fool-able, and hilarious. (Actually, that was taken from a blurb on the back cover of one of her books.) She's like those fast-talking Hollywood studio stars from the 1950s who spoke in movie lines: "I'm tired of getting the fuzzy end of the lollipop" or "Fasten your seat belt, it's going to be a bumpy ride!"

Annabelle had written a piece for the *New York Times* that I assumed would be in the manner of her nonfiction books. She's written such books as *You Say Tomato, I Say Shut Up*—which gives you a taste of her wit. I was expecting a pithy romp from her. I got the opposite.

Annabelle had a persistent cough during the pandemic. And due to her fear of doctors and lack of health insurance, she delayed getting a Covid test. She finally pulled into an urgent care in Los Angeles to discover she did not have Covid-19 (phew), but did have stage-four lung cancer (What the fuck). STAGE-FOUR LUNG CANCER!

Without hesitation I emailed her. I felt deeply heartsick. I consider her a one-of-my-people kinda gal. A woman with whom I felt a kinship even though we were no longer in communication and lived on separate coasts. I was praying she was in remission.

I couldn't stop thinking about Annabelle while I waited for her to reply. I had a consistent pit in my stomach. Naturally, I had to unpack all the feelings of "this could be me." It sounds narcissistic, but you can't help but think that way; it's hardwired into our DNA.

Every summer in Chatham, Massachusetts, there is a great white shark sighting. And every summer I wake up in a night terror because I know that particular shark is hunting me. Any Lifetime movie about a man who cheats on his wife—yup, I cast my husband. If there's a global pandemic, I get the virus. Wait, that did happen. When I had Covid, I had heart-racing nightmares about lung cancer. Having never experienced such respiratory distress before, even when I had pneumonia, I didn't feel it was beyond the realm of possibility. Maybe because of the similarities in our careers or maybe because we both were once social cigarette smokers,

I couldn't shake the idea that lung cancer could be in the cards for me as well.

Annabelle had no idea she was sick! She was dealing with a divorce and financial stress. There was not a trace of a life-threatening disease! She saw no great white fin in the water . . . and if she hadn't gone for a Covid test (in a mini-mall next to a Trader Joe's), would she ever have known?

And how would I know if I had . . . Wait. This is about Annabelle. Not my own personal fear of the C-word. And she is a force. And a woman of great wisdom. Not a sub-scriber to the *how you can see cancer as a gift* line of bullshit. So I had to know how she faced her own mortality. I needed to learn from her.

It's fascinating how people deal with other people's hard-ships. For example, I just made it about me! But there should be a handbook. In the *Times* piece, Annabelle said during Covid her neighbors left her a single glass of wine in the bushes at night. Cozy, yet slightly odd. What if a squirrel had found it? What would the fate of a drunk squirrel be? I guess roadkill. Another friend gave Annabelle a juicer. Juices are supposed to cure all. Listen, I drink tons of juice. I still have cellulite! And a bloated gut. And juice didn't thwart the cyst from devouring my ovary. Annabelle's juicer has yet to be taken out of the box. She was told to eat raw food, see a psychic surgeon, and watch TED Talks about people with cancer who ran marathons. People get compulsive about fixing the problem. Apparently, you can eradicate ringworm with parsnip puree. And the tremendous thing about Annabelle is she isn't having any of it. She doesn't want to run a marathon or be applauded for lofty postdiagnosis ambitions postdiagnosis. She will take her pills and do what the doctors tell her to do. Nothing more, nothing less. No bucket lists. What she does do is live her normal life. Every day. And that's enough. Even though she was getting divorced, had no health insurance, was about to lose her house, no employment, and we were in a global pandemic! . . . I would have never gotten out of bed.

Annabelle should be handed the Peabody or Pulitzer or an award with a big, gold statue for how she has faced this crisis with fortitude and positivity. She has kept her masterly sense of humor intact. As I realized one day when I finally got up the nerve to call her. I asked her what keeps her from falling into the depths of a dark depression with what-all she was dealing with, and she buoyantly answered, "Oh! I started Zoom ukulele lessons with two friends." I was not expecting that answer. And she was pretty certain they would get so professional-sounding that their group would turn into a celebrated band. They were concentrating on R.E.M. songs. "The spirited thing about ukulele band practice," she told me, "is we're all together, laughing and focusing on the activity of this music (however good or bad). And nobody has to talk about their lives, the news, or my diagnosis." It turns out that ukuleles are like kittens. Joy makers.

It would annoy Annabelle if I touted her mindset as empowering, particularly for people who are suffering with devastating health issues. But tough shit, Annabelle, it's true. A sense of humor is a saving grace for some people. You either have one or you don't. And if you don't, hopefully you can appreciate someone who does. But it is Annabelle's ability to find the absurdity in a cancer diagnosis and her honesty about it that impress and inspire me the most.

Get ready—I'm about to say something so "cringe" (as the youngsters like to say) and cliché it may cause you to throw this book against the fridge . . . "Life is a gift; wake up every day and realize that." I know, I know. But there's a reason we all gravitate toward quote-of-the-day calendars, Aristotle, and the film *Billy Elliot*! Without aspiration, we don't have the ability to seek out the best versions of ourselves. I think about times when I've had the flu, or debilitating surgery or Covid. I want to will myself healthy. And I'm confounded by how much I take my health for granted when I am hearty and strong. I promise myself that when I'm recovered, I will never take a robust and vigorous life for granted.

Annabelle (putting aside the enormous amount of sidelined difficulties) is told she has stage-four lung cancer and, instead of crumbling, decides to take a ukulele class. And enjoy every second of it. She didn't just seize the day, she seized the life.

I unpacked my emergency art purchases. And I painted. With blues and greens. It won't hang in the National Gallery or set records someday at Sotheby's. It's complete crap. But the smell of acrylic paint . . . the glass jar filled with muddled water. The art is in the doing.

Unhappy Birthday to You

During the pandemic I found that there were times when we needed a bit of magic. A happiness bump, if you will. During moments of low-level, nonspecific despair, a sense of isolation that comes from being apart from your friends and loved ones, with no end in sight . . . in such cases, I would make the thirty-minute trek to Carvel. And purchase what I can only call a little bit of fairy dust. The holy grail of ice cream cakes, in the shape of a whale. With a crunchy center. There's a base of vanilla ice cream, topped with a generous band of chocolate cookie crunchies, which in turn is topped with chocolate ice cream, which is covered in a glossy fudge icing with frozen whipped cream frosting piped thickly around the border. The outside edges are coated in more chocolate crunchies, and there is a face drawn on with more white frosting piping: an eyebrow, an eye, and a smiling mouth, although their particular form, tail size, and resulting expression vary widely. You might get a smiling or bewildered Fudgie, or a somewhat maniacal-looking iteration, but the taste is consistent.

Fudgie the whale got us through some very dark times. Sometimes we would harpoon the whale with our forks without even taking it out of the box. After all, you should never eat more than you can lift. And suddenly there would be laughter. Yes, I know skeptics will chalk our gaiety up to all that processed sugar, but I am convinced of the mystical effects of that particular ice cream cake. It was not only a party in your mouth, but for me it was also edible nostalgia. And let's not forget the fact that Tom Carvel, who was the founder, was actually Greek (formerly known as Athanasios Thomas Karvelas). If you marry a Greek, as I have, you are married to all Greeks. So Tom Carvel is actually my ex-husband.

Fudgie is adaptable. At Christmastime, he's flipped on his head and cloaked in red-and-white frosting to stand in for Santa Claus. On Father's Day, the piping reads *Have a whale of a Father's Day*, but if you request a female Fudgie for Mother's Day, you get one with pink piping, icing eyelashes, and a little bow. Over fifty thousand Fudgie the Whale cakes are sold a year. Forty-three thousand to me. In the past two years. During your next existential crisis, before you call a therapist or try MDMA, reach for a Fudgie the Whale.

Plastics

I just want to say one word to you . . . just one word . . . are you listening? Plastics! There is a great future in plastics!" One of the great lines from the classic film *The Graduate*. "And there is a great future in plastic . . . surgery," I overheard once in the Houston airport.

I had burrowed into our sofa like a groundhog, where I remained most of the winter. With a heated blanket. Covered in crumbs. One afternoon (pick any day in March) I was reading a *New Yorker* article about how women were clamoring for face-lifts during the pandemic. Hmmm . . . weren't doctors busy enough saving lives? Some women were saying, *Why the hell not?*—your recovery time was infinite because the world was in lockdown.

It made me laugh. The idea that during such a horrific time in history, people were worried about crow's-feet! That people were begging doctors to perform these surgeries during a peak in Covid cases struck me as less funny. The plastic surgeons flatly refused, which led the potential patients to offer four times the price—one doctor was even offered to be flown on a private jet to the Middle East! What was wrong with these people?

Perhaps there was something I wasn't getting. As a human, I just wanted to stay alive! And to allow myself every comfort that the oppressive times offered. Hence the heated blanket and the high cholesterol. Did this community have some secret intel that when the pandemic is over only the beautiful will have survived? Was there some master-race plot to weed out the undesirables and spare only models and Instagram influencers?

I tried to look at it another way. People needed to feel in control. Any way they could. And there was so little one could control. People were losing jobs, housing, getting divorced (but still stuck in the same space). There was nothing reliable. You couldn't bank on anything. Maybe for the people who could afford such lavish procedures, they were investing in themselves. Or maybe it was just plain ole narcissism.

I did not invest in myself. I did the opposite. I got depressed and watched my hair fall out in clumps. As my family and I slurped on minestrone soup, I couldn't help but make jokes about the women so desperate for nip/tucks. I imagined them in designer hazmat suits banging on the glass doors of plastic surgery offices in Beverly Hills and Palm Beach. Or a group of them in black jumpsuits throwing a blanket over a renowned rhinoplasty doctor and shoving him into the back of a windowless van.

—

Zoom. Zoom Zoom Zoom-a Zoom. Zoom was a complicated, high-concept phenomenon when I first started receiving links. And I thought FaceTime required a Princeton degree. I had just perfected the ability to post on Instagram when Zoom came on the scene. Don't even ask me to set up a proper Zoom room. At the beginning of it all, I was still burrowed in the sofa with dimmed lights so the screen was relatively dark. I looked like someone in witness protection or a turned Islamic fundamentalist being interviewed on *20/20*. And because of spotty Wi-Fi, I was blurry most of the time. But then the seasons changed and the sun appeared like one gigantic halogen floodlight. And in the bright bulb of summer, I started spiraling down the tunnel of Zoom face dysmorphia.

I never wore sunscreen. It was not a thing when I was a kid. Or if it was, I don't remember my mother slathering it on us. The only things you took to the beach were a tattered, mildewy towel and a mayonnaise sandwich. When you got your driver's license, you tilted your face out the window to soak up rays and let your freak hair fly. The whole point of spring break was to get baked. That's why you wrapped your record album in tinfoil for optimum rays. So, consequently, after all my toasting and roasting, I have the sun damage to show for it. And I will have to live with a constellation of brown sun spots on my skin for the rest of my life. And the memory of my daughters as toddlers asking me why the specks of dirt would not wash off my face. The little darlings . . .

But I have done nothing to deserve a droopy neck! Based on old photographs of my grandparents, it seems to have been one of the traits handed down, like scoliosis and glaucoma. It's as if somebody unsnapped my taut jowls, like a bra, and they just dropped. Overnight! It's been a long time since I took physics, but I remember a basic law, the gist of which is that when one thing drops, another is propelled upward—like if you dumped a bag of sand on one end of a seesaw. In my case, there were two bags of sand dropped on both sides of the seesaw and then the seesaw broke.

The first few sunlit Zooms, I watched myself fiddle with the crepey skin. How the fuck did I get so old so fast? Was it a pandemic thing?

After a few weeks, I could barely focus on what was discussed during the Zoom meetings. Philanthropy, human connection, mindfulness, blah blah. All I could see was imperfection. As I mentioned before, I have never been fixated on my looks. (Um, yeah, we know, Ali.) I'm "relatable." I have never bleached my teeth. And have always maintained that witty repartee was sexier than hard nipples that point to the sun. So I was enraged by my shallow self-absorption. It's one thing to be the nubile, hot model wearing a size-negative-zero pair of white jeans. She's paid to look like that! It's her job! That's why she only eats radishes and rides the Peloton to Kansas and back. I prided myself on being the antithesis of vanity. My God, I used Nivea body cream on my face! That's how much I didn't care! I've even cut my own hair! So why, why, WHY did I suddenly care that I had grooves as deep as trenches on the sides of my cheeks and enough neck fat to feed a family of five?

My mother always taught me about the evils of vanity. She finds fillers and injections incredibly self-indulgent. Not unlike masturbation. She doesn't wear any makeup, or even lip balm, for that matter. And I have inherited that no-nonsense outlook. I don't wear makeup unless I'm working. Sometimes when I'm on a TV talk show I'll catch a glimpse of myself in the monitor (after a couple hours of hair and makeup) and gasp. Because I don't know who I'm looking at! It's Ali 2.0. But an impossible way to live day-to-day unless I have a village of professionals walking in front of me with lighting, a powder brush, mirrors, and a smoke machine.

So the fact that I found myself browsing plastic surgery websites during the pandemic was truly disconcerting. For fuck's sake, why don't I use that time to write a novel or organize the spice drawer? This is so vacuous. Scroll, scroll, scroll . . . oh! Look at Glenn Close's milky, taut neck! I started to compare surgeons by their patients' before and after photos. I would ooooh and aaaah as if watching a magic trick; sometimes I even applauded. I studied the photos so meticulously, if someone had bought me a surgery kit and a magnifying mirror I could have performed a neck lift in the comfort of my home.

When things began to open up, women emerged jogging on the streets and picking up green juice curbside, heavily masked and within six feet of one another (too far to whisper, *Hey, who did your brow lift?*). Everyone was still sporting sweatpants whether they exercised or not. But hair was back to being colored, and small amounts of mascara were being applied. It was like watching live-action evolution. But the masks still hid most of the faces. Something I hope we never do away with.

I was walking Cooper in the park when I spotted a woman in a tangerine tracksuit coming toward me. She was fast-walking with earbuds and attitude. Just as she whipped by, she stopped and turned.

I had no clue who it was. She was wearing a mask the size of a diaper. It turns out we'd worked together at a nonprofit years ago before she married a wealthy contractor. As we were outside, she pulled off her mask to gulp some fresh air.

I am not exaggerating when I say that it was a completely

different person standing in front of me. This was not the woman I recalled in a smock dress trying to figure out how to get local subsidies to pay for free school lunches in underserved neighborhoods.

"You look exactly the same, Ali."

I scrunched my un-Botoxed brow. "You look so . . . different!"

She gleefully regaled me with her soup-to-nuts surgery makeover story. She'd had eye, nose, tummy, lip, and facelifts. She'd had fat sucked out of her ass and injected into her cheeks and lips and God knows where else. The only thing she hadn't done was a Brazilian butt lift. Otherwise, because of the tummy tuck, she would have had to sleep standing up. I imagined her spending months covered in gauze and the slow unveiling party. If that's a thing. And I was proud of myself. I didn't fall prey to the media and consumer capitalist brainwashing of the importance of a youthful facade. I'd earned my muffin top and wrinkles. Especially from the last two years. They were my war wounds (I'm including scars from childbirth in that).

And yet, as we said our goodbyes, the words seemed to slip from my mouth involuntarily. "Just curious . . . who's your doctor?"

Listen, as Jean Kerr once said, "I'm tired of all this nonsense about beauty being only skin deep. That's deep enough. What do you want—an adorable pancreas?"

Hidden
Treasure

No human, mammal, reptile, or amphibian should spend all day and all night with their mate. Bees, sharks, and snakes (as intertwined as they are) require alone time to hunt, feed, or just get a breath of fresh air or water. Even cave people knew to go their separate ways to hunt and gather or stoke the fires and skin the meat. Solitude is essential to one's mental stability.

So suddenly things stop. And we are in lockdown. And we mammals have to downshift into hibernation mode. Except there's one problem—we won't be asleep for six months like the bears. We will be hibernating and wide awake. And for more than six months, as it turns out.

We were at the point where eating with an open mouth, grinding teeth, snoring—all of which were once easy enough to overlook—suddenly became intolerable. I'm sure I drove my husband bananas too! Although I can't come up with one character flaw . . . I, however, trumpeted my dissatisfaction with the way he loaded the dishwasher, the accumulation of boxers on the floor, and the fact that he never closes the cabinet doors. I like to call those moments the "snappy" moments, because you don't actually quarrel, you snap. And snapping turns to festering, and festering turns to full-on blowups. And the blowups are intense and nuclear, and then you don't remember what you're fighting about. Then the storm is downgraded to snappiness once again. It's like blowing up a balloon and then letting the air out. Over and over.

Everyone was always searching for a nook in which to hide. The teenagers knew their rooms were private temples. We were forbidden entry without knocking and pleading. They needed to recharge regularly in their catacombs with their computers and phones. The shades were down, the lights were off, and they were cocooned under their down comforters. Their rooms were about as inviting as a morgue.

My husband and I played human chess around the kitchen and our bedroom, searching for solitude in a quiet corner. A closet. A trunk. A bathtub. To do something, anything, or nothing. My husband was deep in the political well of online news, gasping at breaking stories. I needed a respite from all that. So I watched anything on TV. And I mean ANYTHING. I'm talking *The Young and the Restless* reruns from the 1980s.

It got to the point where my limbs were close to atrophy. It was freezing outside, so I couldn't chop wood or build a barn. It was too crowded in the house to sledgehammer walls or build a masonry chimney. So I went to the basement looking for escape. And a storage closet to transform into my new living quarters. I noticed large amounts of mouse poop, but the idea of setting traps (humane ones) felt too depressing. I'm sure the mice were struggling with their own pandemic ordeals. Black mold? Out of my expertise, plus I only sneeze when I'm really close to that part of the floor. I did find Container Store plastic bins stuffed with Christmas ornaments, stockings, and decorations. Finally, something character building that would give me a sense of purpose.

I removed every ornament, bit of yellowed tissue paper, and broken Santa head from the bins and vacuumed the bottoms. I could hear the clinking of the ornament hooks scraping the sides of the hose. I gingerly wrapped every glass candy cane and snowflake in paper towels. The photo frame ornaments made me emotional, and when I pulled up the Popsicle-stick figures of Jesus, Joseph, and Mary my daughter had made, I fell to the cold cement floor, weeping and inhaling black mold.

I took a break before tackling the old Easter baskets and went upstairs for a snack. I found some stale Sour Patch

Kids, which required twenty minutes of chewing to make it down my throat. When I went to stuff the bag of candy back under the sink, I stood up too quickly and hit my head on a cabinet door. I screamed things that would cause my mother to faint (and she worked in politics). The crown of my head throbbed so badly I checked for blood.

What was it about my husband and cabinet doors? At this point, it had to be purposeful: I have told him over and over for twenty years at least three times a day not to leave the damn doors open!!!! Three times a day multiplied by 365 days multiplied by twenty years equals 21,900. 21,900 times I have reminded him to please close the cabinet doors. And yet, during the global plague of our lifetime, when no doctor is available to treat my cracked skull, he grabs his granola and LEAVES THE DOOR WIDE OPEN! I decided to just bleed out. Well, there was no blood but I'm sure irreparable damage. I couldn't spell my married last name! (Not that anyone can.)

I stomped down the basement steps. I figured I would eventually hemorrhage next to the mice droppings. Nobody will notice I'm missing until they realized the chicken tacos aren't on the dinner table.

The Easter basket job took less than ten minutes. I think when you've reorganized your seasonal decorations, you've reached a level of idleness that can't get any lower. Oh, wait!

I found a large apothecary jar of colored pens. I decided to check each pen to see if there was still ink. I created a save and throw-away pile. Okay, it got lower. When I had completed that imperative and time-sensitive chore, I noticed a moldy box with ancient shipping tape across it. It had my husband's initials faintly scrolled on the side. Now, let me just add here—we have moved many, many times in our twenty-year marriage. New York. Washington, DC. Back to New York. Different apartments. New baby—bigger apartment. Another new baby—even bigger apartment. So I have packed and unpacked boxes and bags more times than a drug cartel. Yes, we lost a few items in some of the moves, most notably my Farrah Fawcett autograph, but overall I was the overseer of every object that was swaddled in Bubble Wrap and tossed into cardboard receptacles. That particular box, however, was unfamiliar. I always marked each box with its owner's first name and what room it belonged in. How had this slippery fella crossed state lines a few times without me clocking it and, more important, ripping it open? How had I left a stone unturned!

My husband likes to throw everything away. "Honey, where are the doctor's instructions on my post-op wound?"

"I threw them out!"

"Have you seen all the girls' artwork from kindergarten to senior year?"

"I threw it out!"

"Sweetheart, do you have our wedding license?"

You get the idea.

Before each move he usually tosses most of his belongings and I end up packing only a couple wardrobe boxes of suits and sweat pants with his name on them. Well, and his thousands of books. He should live in the public library with a futon and a hot plate.

As I opened the box, the tape deteriorated in my hands. And like a character from *The Mummy*, I held a photo of him from college up to the light like it was the lost Ark. There he was in very short shorts, tan, with a shag haircut, arm around another teenage boy, in what looked like a foreign land. More blurry photos from the 1970s. Then another photo of him, pudgy on his mother's lap. It was a treasure trove. Old driver's licenses, awards, his Columbia diploma. A stack of magazine covers and articles about his meteoric rise in politics. Maybe he had been hiding it from me because he was building a secret time capsule?

Underneath was a stack of cards and letters. I braced myself. They looked like love letters. I assumed from ghosts of girlfriends past. I saw a couple hearts. *But the past is the past*, I told myself. I have old letters and photos of relationships that played an integral part in who I am today. I mean, I have dated some pretty, pretty hot guys. Yet it was not okay for my husband to have a past. A double standard? Yes.

But I believe in double standards when they work in my favor.

My heart was beating. What if I found a nude photo in that box? I would have to risk Covid, get in the car, and drive to Santa Fe. I say Santa Fe because I've always equated it with a destination for people trying to escape trauma. I pictured myself in an adobe house with a three-legged dog and lots of chunky turquoise jewelry. Spirituality, incense, and enchiladas. Actually, that sounded like heaven.

Anyway, no nudies. I started to dig through the cards. They were mine! I had written them! One card I had hand-delivered on the eve of our wedding. Our first anniversary letter. Valentine's Day cards. I always make my valentines with photos, glue glitter, paint, and the imagination of a nine-year-old.

He had saved every piece of correspondence. It was like a box of his life! If Armageddon hit (or global warming) and an alien population inhabited earth and one of the aliens purchased our house (for more than we'd paid because I'd renovated) and found the box . . . they would know who my husband was. Sure, where he'd gone to school and all the Wikipedia-type information, but also the kind of love he'd lived. The alien would take its green, webbed flippers and trace the words and the hearts and maybe even eat the glitter. He might be a little confused, because hearts were the equivalent of poop emojis in his alien world. But he would feel it. He would know in his reptilian gut that there was joy and passion and something beautiful in that box.

I thought about the cabinet door. And the bump on my head. How petty and irrelevant it was to fight about the insignificant things. I thought about how on our second date when we kissed outside on a spring night in the West Village he tasted like vodka and lime. How he always takes my hand when we walk or sit across from each other at dinner. And how I still catch him gazing at me sometimes with such amour it makes my cheeks flush.

I love him. Truly and forever. And here we were in a home we created, with two daughters who embodied the best of both of us, a hound who howled around the clock, and an obese dachshund. In a pandemic. So why would I spend another minute snapping at this man who had given me such a rich life? If the news had shown me anything, it's that life is short and unpredictable. Sorry to sound like something you read next to the toilet. But it's true. And I don't know how else to describe it without a flute, a long white scarf, and ballet shoes.

I packed up the box, worthless tape and all, and pushed it to the back of storage. Saving it for the aliens.

Upstairs my husband was making coffee in the kitchen. There were two cabinet doors open. I smiled as I closed them softly, taking care not to slam them. I walked over to him as he pressed down the top of the French coffeepot. I wrapped my arms around him and squeezed. He turned and we kissed, I mean KISSED, like we did that second date on Irving Place. And for the first time since the world was ravaged by an unknown virus, I felt safe. I didn't need any distraction from this moment.

Deliverance

Like an obstinate oyster, the country had finally opened. Life seemed somewhat normal. Aside from everyone wearing a mask or a brawl breaking out if someone didn't. That was not normal. But all in all, the landscape was starting to look familiar.

I have, for the past decade, gone away every weekend of my birthday. I look forward to it all year. Many of my friends will say, "You go away ALONE? On your BIRTH-DAY?" Yes, I do. And I come back a better wife, mother, and human. I can sleep late without anyone nudging my foot for cash, wanting sex, needing to go out and pee . . . (insert kid, husband, and dog in any of these). I can breathe! I can actually think. You forget how we are constantly bombarded during the day! Mostly by texts.

And no, I'm not scared traveling solo. Even though the internet is filled with disturbing tales about single women being killed in resorts or out jogging or standing on a cliff taking selfies. But it's always the husband. And by the way—why do they kill their wives? Why not divorce them? As much as the husbands fake plead and weep on the local news, they inevitably get caught and serve a life sentence. For what? Because they didn't want her to receive alimony? Don't put your wife in a wood chipper, call a lawyer.

Anyway, my birthday is in January. But since we were all in the throes of the pandemic, and my whole family lived in one bed like some *Willy Wonka & the Chocolate Factory* reboot directed by David Lynch, I did not go away on my annual birthday trip.

April was different. We could travel domestically. And if there was any year when I needed that weekend, it was 2021. I started Googling "middle-aged female solo trips." The only results were a Sandals resort and a retirement village in Boca. As I surfed Expedia, one of my closest friends, Maggie, called and suggested we do a girls' trip with another friend of ours, Bette. Everyone needed an escape. Mostly from teenagers. And we'd stay in a place with room service, where we didn't have to make the bed. Or do laundry. And we'd talk to humans other than our families.

I love my women friends. I would run naked in a circle and howl under a full moon if anyone were game. One time they were. But that's another book.

"Let's go to the woods!" I declared even though I have

a propensity toward water. I had heard about this retreat in the mountains of Tennessee. I had spent hours poring over their website's gallery of hiking trails, close-up shots of berries, and lots of sage bundles. They claimed to have infused wellness. I love anything infused!

We reached the lodge after a full day of Covid-restricted airports and rental cars. I thought about the irony of when, in years past, I would see the occasional traveler wearing a mask and think, *Oh, come on, isn't that a little extreme?* Turns out the joke was on me.

It was eerie being disconnected from my family and surrounded by mountains and strangers. The refuge sat on thousands of acres in the midst of the Great Smoky Mountains. Dense forest, wildflowers, and caramel-colored stone houses. You wouldn't call us "country girls"; more like "city girls who bought cowboy hats and bandanas solely for that trip." Bette had fractured her knee a few months earlier, so she wobbled around like an inebriated Tiny Tim. Her fantasy was to read *Manifesting through Meditation* by the fire as Maggie and I dropped forty pounds in two days. With all the infused stuff. As we checked in, we fielded the 438 texts that had come in from our children. Mine were all about how one of the dogs had diarrhea all over the living room and they didn't want to make a mistake cleaning it up, so they were just going to leave it for me for when I got back. Little angels; it felt like Mother's Day! Maggie was coordinating school pickups, and Bette was whispering about how to get blood out of silk.

We finally collapsed on the floor of our woodsy cabin, a little three-bedroom cottage tucked away in a massive cluster of pine trees. All was cozy and copacetic until we realized that the three bedrooms were all completely different. One had a maple four-poster bed with windows overlooking a babbling brook and grassy knoll. The second bedroom was like a guest room at your grandma's, complete with pastel sheets and a needlepoint chair seat. The third bedroom was the size of a coat closet with a tiny window overlooking the street. We declared that bedroom the shithole. And if you knew how much we were spending for that weekend, you would have too. Then came the awkward twenty-minute discussion about where everyone was going to sleep.

"Maybe because of my knee I should just stay on this floor so no stairs?" The beautiful master bedroom with the maple bed was on the first floor.

"Good point, but it's a long walk to the bathroom with the giant freestanding bathtub, so maybe you should take one of the two bedrooms upstairs?"

"Sure. I could. But I know you get spooked at night, so wouldn't you feel safer upstairs, away from the front door?"

I cut in. "Let's just decide like mature adults. I'm tearing up paper and putting three numbers in a bowl."

The number one was for the master, two was the guest

room, and three was the shithole. When we all picked, Bette got the shit room. It didn't seem fair. Well, not to her. Maggie and I thought it was fair. We were all splitting the trip three ways, so in the end, we decided to round-robin the bedrooms. We would each get a night in all of the bedrooms. Translation: nobody could escape the shithole.

Our first evening was spent at the lodge restaurant. Everything was labeled "artisanal." Cheese boards, Calabrian chilis, pickled pears, locally farmed greens. All of them non-industrial and handcrafted. Maggie and Bette drank elderberry martinis as we inhaled a sweet potato pizza with kale and rosemary. We hobbled back to our cabin with flashlights and a sense of ebullience. After getting into pajamas, we chewed on melatonin gummies and tumbled into the crisp, clean sheets of our designated beds. (Even the shithole's sheets were 1200-thread-count Egyptian cotton.)

The next afternoon, Maggie and I decided we should go on a hike. After all, we were in the mountains, and all the other guests wore hiking boots and olive-green sports gear. Lying around in our pajamas drinking coffee and telling old boyfriend sex stories was too reminiscent of the months of Covid. We needed to take advantage of nature. And acquire muscle mass again.

We walked to the top of the hill near the main lodge to a trail I had circled on our resort map. It was a one-hour hiking loop. For seniors and pregnant women. We couldn't find the start of the trail, so we asked a young, long-haired dude, who looked like an extra from *Bill & Ted's Excellent Adventure*. Even though he was employed by the resort and wore khaki shorts and a white polo shirt with a name tag, he hadn't a clue. Well, he hadn't a clue in general. We asked a second employee, in the same uniform and a little more coherent, who pointed to a bunch of trees.

As we started down the rocky path, he yelled out, "Watch out for rattlers and copperheads!"

We froze. My number one fear is reserved for sharks. But snakes place a close second. Snakes, to me, are just sharks on land. You don't see them coming until they lunge at you with open mouths and gnarly teeth.

I kept this line of thinking to myself as we started down the dirt path. Walking in a terrain we knew was infested with poisonous snakes. I guess the idea of tightening our asses outweighed the fear of being bitten by a venomous serpent and having less than forty-five minutes to live.

I stomped, like my husband does when he can't find his cell phone, so the vibrations would scare off the snakes. After about twenty minutes, as the towering pine trees enveloped us, we forgot about vipers and turned to gut health and psychotherapy, yapping about probiotics, stopping occasionally to admire a swooping hawk or a bunch of bluebells.

And then we came to a fork in the path. Yes, this is also a metaphor. I was adamant about turning right. Maggie disagreed but, against her better judgment, relented, and we made our way toward a rather steep hill. I was certain that when we got to the top we would descend down to the lodge, where we would reward ourselves with cold mint lemonade. But when we finally (gasping and sweating) reached the peak, we saw nothing. No structures of any kind. Just woods, woods, and more woods.

We had been hiking over an hour and a half by now. Maggie decided it was time for Google Maps. Whoops—no cell service. In these modern times, no bars on your phone is the equivalent of running out of oxygen. The panic set in.

We kept trudging through weeds, rocks, and poison oak. There were no trail signs of any kind. No arrows, trail markers, or bread crumbs. We kept walking. And walking. Finally, we saw a tiny bit of stone peeking through the birch trees. *Phew.*

We sprinted toward the stone structure, fantasizing about the enormous cheddar burgers with pickled onions on artisanal buns we were going to inhale. As we neared the building, however, we realized it was a single home. An isolated house in the woods and not part of the resort.

"Somebody will be home, and we'll ask to use their phone," I optimistically predicted. "Serial killers don't have fountains with cement birds and squirrels."

We knocked on a few windows. Nothing. Not even a yapping terrier or menacing cat. So we quietly walked across the nicely appointed patio with painted ladybug sculptures and plastic sunflowers, down the driveway—to be met with a wrought iron gate. Maggie gamely attempted to scale it. She kept hoisting herself up to the top but was unable to vault her body over the final tips. As she was making her eighteenth try, I noticed there were two pathways bookending the gate. So we simply walked around it. Poor security planning.

We wandered down the road. A newly paved road. There were no other homes, cars, signs of life. I can't remember even hearing the chirp of a bird. As we started to really hoof it, we held our cell phones up to the sky as if the higher they were, the better the chance that God or Verizon would save us. In hindsight, it's even more ridiculous than it felt at the time. Maggie and I are middle-aged women who need reading glasses to see anything. The idea that we would know how to ping or track or share our location is on par with us performing triple bypass surgery. My teenage daughters have apps where they can detect the exact location of every one of their friends at any given second. I can barely power my phone off.

We decided to sprint. Dusk was approaching, and everyone knows that when the sun goes down, bad shit happens.

"It's getting twilighty! I think that's when the bears come out!" I wheezed, trotting next to her.

"WHAT?! Is that true?"

"I feel like it's true! Didn't you read *National Geographic* when you were a kid?"

Maggie upped her pace. "If we see a bear, what do we do?" She scanned the area as if we were soldiers behind enemy lines.

"You get into a ball and don't move," I said confidently (pulling the fact out of my ass).

"I thought you were supposed to make a ton of noise and act big," she said, holding her arms outstretched.

"I thought that was grizzlies."

"What are here?"

"Black bears, right?"

"Grizzlies are out west?"

"Wasn't Yogi Bear a grizzly? He was out west, right?"

"So what bears are in the circus?"

"Shit, I can't remember . . . I think they are different in America as opposed to the Russian circus."

"What's the difference?"

"One is brown, and one is black . . . but I think they both maul and kill!"

We started running faster. Finally, we saw a sign of life: a dilapidated, burned-out shack. Most of the base was left, but the roof was gone and most of the walls deteriorated. The rest was charred logs. There was a sign nailed to a tree— BEWARE OF DOG. And then we heard music playing from a radio. We couldn't see where it was coming from. It was acid rock. Satan-worshipping-type music.

"It's a meth lab," I whispered.

"How do you know what a meth lab looks like?" She stopped to catch her breath.

"Propane tanks—obviously one of them caused an explosion. And smell that odor—doesn't it smell like pee after you've taken a ton of vitamins? Plus, a BEWARE OF DOG sign?"

You know when you're in danger. It's a primal feeling that bolts through your whole body. Your heart beats faster, your armpits sting, and the tendons on the backs of your knees start to quiver. You may not pay attention to it, but it's there. When you sense someone following you in the shopping mall parking lot, when the German shepherd breaks from its leash, when you're walking down the aisle in a wedding dress about to marry someone you don't love.

We both had that feeling. And we expeditiously snapped into fight-or-flight mode. Holding hands, we started charging down the road. I'd seen enough episodes of *Law & Order: SVU* to know how this could potentially end.

A black pickup truck appeared in the distance. Oh, thank God. An end to this low-budget horror film. We waved at the truck. And waved more vigorously the closer it got. It sped by us as we jumped out of the way. Then it screeched to a halt and abruptly reversed back to us, spraying gravel everywhere. The driver was covered in tattoos and had a cigarette dangling from his lips. He wore a baseball cap and dark glasses. A casting director might have dismissed him as too cliché for the predator role in our nightmare.

"Y'all okay?" He gave us a full look-over. Like he was choosing between rib eye or New York strip.

"We're fine," I gasped, a forced smile plastered on my face. At that point, I would rather have been torn apart by the razor-sharp claws of a bear than risk getting into that truck.

He peeled off and we rocketed forward. I tried to imagine a helicopter, Idris Elba at the controls, throwing down a rope for us, which we caught in one try, dangling over the misty hills and lakes to safety.

I had no idea my body was capable of that kind of Herculean strength. I don't run. Even for the subway or a late flight. But that afternoon I could have run the New York City Marathon.

And then we saw it. Her. Him. Them. WE SAW A BLACK BEAR! About fifty feet from us. A big, charcoal-colored, hungry (I assume) bear. Rambling along the opening of the woods just off the road. We stopped. The bear stopped. We stopped breathing. He kept breathing. Then the bear slowly lumbered by us until it was a shadow disappearing into the foliage. HOLY SHIT!

The only time I had ever seen a bear in the wild was years ago when my husband and I took our kids camping in Canada. One afternoon we'd ventured out in a dinghy with a guide motoring through the water between uninhabited islets when we spotted a bear cub.

"A baby bear! Look, girls, it's Paddington!"

We turned off the motor and peacefully drifted as we watched the cub scamper up a mammoth pine tree.

"Aw, look! He's playing!"

Suddenly, a large adult bear came barreling toward the baby bear in the tree.

"There's the mommy! See? They're playing hide-and-seek just like we do at home!"

We smiled and took photos. A bear cub in a tree? That's a million likes on Instagram!

Our guide said calmly, "Oh, that's not the mother bear, that's the father bear. The males need to pass on their DNA, which is why they try to spread their seed to every female. So male bears will sometimes kill the cubs, forcing the female's body to stop lactating and shift back into re-production mode. That's what's going on here. He's trying to kill that little cub."

My children began to wail.

"Maybe we can get out of here?" The guide just sat there, like a statue, watching the imminent brutal murder.

Finally, the screaming girls appeared to jolt him out of his reverie, and he started the motor. We sped off before we could be traumatized for the rest of our lives. And I spent the next few years reassuring them, "No! Humans don't eat their young! Don't be scared of Daddy!"

And here I was once again on vacation with a bear. And if I've learned anything, it's where there's one, there're more . . .

We started running again, but at this point we were exhausted and falling over each other. It was as if our bodies had given out, but our feet were like, *Are you fucking nuts? We're getting the hell out of here!*

Maggie suddenly tripped. Her ankle rolled, and she flew forward onto her hands and knees. She was in excruciating pain. We had reached the point in the horror movie when it's nightfall and one of the girls needs medical attention and bad decisions are made, like "Let's go back to the burnt-out house and see if the serial killer skinning animals can move his meat hooks aside and help us."

We were at our most vulnerable and losing hope.

A Volvo. A cream-colored 1990s Volvo careened around the bend. Because Maggie was sitting on the road clutching her knees, visibly in distress, the car stopped. The window went down, and we saw two old faces. They looked like Santa and Mrs. Claus. I was not going to let these kind folks leave without us. Even if I had to throw Maggie on the hood.

The grandma opened the door, and we piled into the back of the car. I mean, a homicidal maniac or a deranged cannibal is not going to drive a Volvo. A Mazda, maybe, but not a Volvo.

It was literally the blind (the driver said he had glaucoma) leading the blind.

They had never heard of the resort we were staying at. And both contradicted each other as to the direction we should take.

"I think we should follow the road down," I suggested. "All things going down lead to something good, like a highway or a body of water or an Arby's." I was practically on Maggie's lap so as not to disrupt the plastic bags of trinkets and whatchamacallits crowding the back seat.

I was hit with an uncomfortable thought: Sometimes in crime stories it's the people nobody suspects. A pearly-haired couple in Holly Hobbie clothing. So affable and God-loving. They offer you a slice of her homemade spiced chocolate chip cookie pumpkin bread . . . and you wake up strapped to a woodworker's table, surrounded by human skin and rusty scythes. I was digging my elbow into Maggie's hip and gesticulating toward the door handle when . . . A sign! A small wooden sign with the lodge's name carved into it with an arrow pointing to the back side of the hideaway.

Bette had been pacing by the front desk for hours. She knew our physical abilities well enough to know we would never be able to withstand more than a forty-five-minute hike. On flat ground. And it had been hours.

After a collective group hug, Bette looked at us. "You guys scared me to death! What if you had seen a bear?!"

We left the resort empty-handed in the rejuvenation department. There were no pledges to drink almond-and-kale smoothies from that day forth. Or read *The Seven Spiritual Laws of Success.* Or do self-regulated mat exercises with Pilates rings. When I got home the next night, I was exhausted. Bruised. Achy. And spent. I had been safer in lockdown. Next year's birthday destination? Anywhere I don't need a venom extractor and bear repellent.

Guess Who's Coming to Dinner

My friend Maggie has a gaggle of kids, a husband, a babysitter, in-laws, and two dogs. When the pandemic hit, they all flocked to Maggie's home, which began to rip at the seams like the proverbial old woman's shoe. Maggie has a cousin, Kyle, who lives alone in downtown Manhattan, who decided to join Maggie and the family as part of their quarantine crew. Except her house was packed. Even though Kyle would have to bed down in his sleeping bag on the kitchen floor, he found comfort in numbers.

Kyle figured that as soon as the pandemic was contained (a week, maybe?), he could return to his bachelor pad with his Phish posters and hot plate. Meanwhile, Maggie's home was starting to resemble the Manson family ranch. I decided, because we had an extra bed, to invite Kyle to stay with us for the week. After all, Maggie and I had agreed to quarantine our families together in a neighborly pod so we weren't breaking protocol.

Kyle arrived wearing Birkenstocks and a Grateful Dead T-shirt. He had the sweetest face, curly apricot-colored hair, and a comforting smile. He held a duffel and his guitar over his shoulder. He reminded me of one of the guys who was in my older brother's band in the 1970s. And by "band," I mean the stoners who practiced in our garage and only got hired once (by our mother, to play at a Democratic fundraiser in our backyard. Mondale lost).

I had gotten to know Kyle over the years, so it wasn't as if a grifter were bunking in with us. He didn't ask for room and board in exchange for some odd jobs around the barn. And we had no chickens for slaughter. I gave him the basement bedroom. No, not what you would imagine a troll trying to hack the Pentagon would dwell in—it's a real guest room set up with a comfortable bed, wooden side tables, and flea market oil paintings of elusive women. I figured it would be seven to ten days, tops. At that point I assumed the pandemic would have run its course the way strep throat does . . .

Secretly, I have always wondered what it would have been like to have had a son. Don't get me wrong: my two daughters are my life. But I will never know the feeling of a son's love for his mother. *Oedipus* has always been my favorite Sophocles play. Yes, he murders his father, but marries his mommy! My little Greek son with brown almond eyes. The spitting image of my husband. And George Clooney. I still see boys running in the park with baseball outfits and I think about how adorable and vivacious they are. Then I think about watching sports games for hours on the bench in the hot sun. And whether to circumcise or not. And then I'm relieved I only have girls. But in 2020 the stork delivered a son to me. A ginger Jew in his early thirties.

Kyle fit in perfectly. His sense of humor. His humbleness. And boy, could he cook. In an apocalyptic plague, the two people you want with you are a doctor and someone who can make meals beyond tuna-fish casserole. Where I saw an old cucumber and a box of rice, Kyle saw a four-star entrée. The night he made his spicy chicken enchiladas was the night we knew he could never leave.

Kyle's most impressive characteristic, aside from his halibut stew, is his surgical wit. He observes the world with a mix of Howard Stern and socialism. And can make us laugh at ourselves even in the most self-absorbed moments. So imagine him with two highly anxious teenage girls in lockdown during a pandemic. The laughter was more uplifting and medicinal than any amount of Wellbutrin.

Parents have a tendency to coddle their children. And by "parents," I mean me. Perhaps it's a reaction to my own WASP childhood, but I'm very physical with my kids. And present. So during the pandemic I practically swaddled my teenage girls and regressed to breastfeeding. It's still a mystery to us that our kids did not get Covid when they had been, literally, on top of me days before I got sick. We needed an outside influence to . . . how can I say this with therapeutic sophistication . . . give them a ton of shit! He would debate them on every political and cultural subject—well, not debate so much as mock. And relish the millions of times the girls told him he was canceled.

Things were not getting better in our country. Kyle was set to venture back to Manhattan. And then I got Covid. And Kyle quarantined with us for three more weeks. And then he just stayed.

Kyle and I bonded very early on. One of the first nights he stayed with us, we watched *Contagion*, an action thriller about a global virus that breaks down societal order as it spreads. A cerebral and realistic film with lines like, "Somewhere in the world, the wrong pig met up with the wrong bat." We should have picked *Hall Pass*. *Contagion* heightened Kyle's already off-the-charts anxiety about the pandemic. He tried to wrap himself in Saran Wrap and place himself in the freezer. "Thaw me out when it's over."

We were all dealing with the situation as cautiously and optimistically as we could. Kyle had a tendency to counter our Pollyanna streak with a little fatalistic data just to keep us on our toes. Our eldest daughter took to her bed like a dethroned ninety-year-old Albanian queen, and my youngest just TikToked. I didn't and still don't fully understand the addiction. I know that some of my kids' friends are "TikTok famous" and that one girl we know got six million hits on her TikTok dancing with her cat. I'm having some trouble keeping up with the times, to be completely honest. I still like black-and-white films with actors like Katharine Hepburn and Veronica Lake. You know, the ones that last longer than three seconds and have a plot? The gray movies, as one of my daughters dubbed them.

Every night at dinner, as the rest of us were dissecting Covid numbers and map graphics, my younger daughter would slowly go into a trance. Silently contorting her arms, flipping her wrists, and moving her neck. She looked like Janis Joplin dropping acid at Woodstock. It didn't happen when we were debating who was the cutest Kardashian baby. And she was capable of lucid conversation about modern-day themes in Jane Austen novels. It was when we discussed anything ominous like, Covid-19, Trump, or menopause.

Then we would lose her. Her eyes would close, her arms floating up above her head, and her torso would start to sway. It was like watching a voodoo exorcism.

My elder daughter decided to make a short film treating the epidemic of TikTok escapism as a modern psychological issue. Kyle played the Freudian shrink, addressing the camera about how it had become a mental health emergency. The film would cut back and forth to my youngest daughter doing her trance dance. The film was very funny, but more important, a much-needed distraction for everyone during some dark winter days. The first day of production commenced in our kitchen. I did secure a cameo as the character called "concerned mom." They wanted a big name like Julianne Moore, but because we were in lockdown and I was the only actor in the house, they had to settle for me. (Apparently, Julianne has shown interest in the sequel.)

As I've mentioned before, my husband was certainly a rock during the pandemic. No question about it. More than a rock. A rock *star*. But with Kyle, I had a playmate. Another adult with stunted growth and the maturity level of a thirteen-year-old. My husband was the person I could be sick with, collapse to, cry on . . . For my children I needed to be steady, maternal, and constantly reassuring. But with Kyle, I could be outrageously and inappropriately funny during the darkest and most unfunny time. My escape was laughter, and he provided it. Sometimes bordering on hysteria.

Kyle and I created characters out of the pure need to escape—two Gen Z characters who say things like "Oh my Gawd" and "Hey Guyzzzz!" We pretended they (our characters) had an Instagram Live show that went live around the clock. We modeled them from the voices of the YouTube videos we would hear my daughters plugged into night after night. We would be making coffee and fall into the characters, "Hey Guyzzzz, we are, like, totally grinding beans for a mochi latte. It's like, super simp to make . . . don't forget to like and subscribe!" We would fall over on the floor giggling. And sometimes we would stay in character for hours until one of my daughters, exasperated, would clap her hands and scream, "STOP!" As an actor, I understand the psychological benefits of recoiling into another persona. At that point, it was much safer than being myself. At that time. In that world.

Something we *could* all agree on was ice cream. My freezer was packed with pints of every form of cookie mash-up. And when we ran low, it was an excuse to escape the house to replenish supplies. To mask up and go out on an adventure to acquire more ice cream. My daughters begged us to take them on long road trips. To anywhere. "Let's just get in the car and drive!" Always an easy NO from us. Unless it was to get ice cream. Ice cream saved us. I also sent ice cream to my parents in Maine and friends in Hudson, New York. It saved them too.

One night, Kyle and my daughter decided to walk into town for . . . yes, ice cream. More specifically, the family favorite, mint chocolate chip. They took a side street that passed by a dilapidated old house. A real teardown. It had shattered windows, a porch missing steps, a rusty chain-link fence. It looked like an *Addams Family* set on the back lot of a Hollywood studio. As they strolled by, they swore they heard an old man scream. "A bloodcurdling wail," as my daughter later reported. Yet they saw nothing but a flicker of a tattered lace curtain on the second floor. They sprinted home full of terror and excitement. And, sadly, no ice cream. We spent the next few months trying to concoct a back-story for the haunted house. We also drove by it almost every night. It became our evening pastime. We'd roll by slowly, looking for signs of life (or death).

Whenever I drive by that house, I silently give thanks. I thank it for providing hours of fantasy and diversion when we needed it most.

Kyle has been living in our house now for over a year. He had a revelation during the pandemic to go back to school to become a social worker and psychotherapist. One can only assume this was born from living with us. He will have to be in the city to attend school in the fall, so there is a hypo-thetical end date. But until then, Kyle plays his guitar in the living room. Smokes his medical marijuana (he claims he has a prescription). Cooks sumptuous seafood stews. And chicken tacos. And brings our family joy. My daughters will always have a surrogate older brother. Kyle will cry at their graduations and tease them about the frivolity of their Sephora purchases. And I will always have a friend, a comrade, who got me through one of the hardest and scariest times in my life. You never know where the angels are until they present themselves.

Homeward Bound, I Wish She Was . . .

My eldest daughter is starting her freshman year at college this fall. And I'm not ready. Empty-nest syndrome is a clinical diagnosis, though I don't recall my mother being so reluctant to let go when I went off to college. Maybe she was just relieved I was actually going to college. I was the third child, and I think the third child is always a roll of the dice. Nobody expects too much of you. You can view the hierarchy of births like this: the firstborn child is heavily studied for croup or lactose intolerance. Every bottle is warmed to 98.6 degrees and tenderly administered in the mother's arms. The second child is given the bottle cold, but still tenderly in the mother's arms. The third child screams for the bottle, which is tossed across the room in hopes of making it into the crib.

My daughter worked very hard for her college acceptance. Her SATs were double what mine were. But you know, in my defense, creative people never do well on standardized tests? There's scientific evidence backing this up. We have a tendency to look at things from a variety of different lenses. In math. And English. History. And languages. I remember there would be some inane paragraph about tigers and a kid named Johnny on the SATs. After reading it, you were asked to circle the box next to the "correct" title of the story. I would instantly think, *Well, if they want to sell books, they should use this title; if they're going for the young adult crowd, they should use this title* . . . And those math problems that asked if Timmy took the train from Pittsburgh, which took two hours, and Danny took the train from Poughkeepsie, how long would . . . all I'd be thinking was, *Borrow a car and drive!*

Chopin and Kandinsky would have gone to state schools, I promise you.

When your child graduates from high school, it is a milestone, even though in truth, the hard work is done the previous year; senior year is just one celebration after another.

Homecomings and proms. Senior skip day—which was every Friday for me in high school. And then graduation day approaches. And although you're busy hemming a polyester gown and looking for sensible heels that won't sink into the grass, there's an undercurrent of melancholy. You stay in denial and occupy yourself with committees setting Covid safety rules for graduation and how to get a decent photo with the seniors wearing masks. Because you're not ready. It's too soon for your child to leave the roost. After all, the roost has fast Wi-Fi, Hulu, and a fully stocked fridge!

Luckily, we didn't have to endure another virtual event when it came to our older daughter's graduation. At the last minute, it was held in Central Park. Socially distanced and with masks. The year before, seniors all over the country were robbed of proms and graduations; homecoming kings and queens missed their moment of crowning glory. Which was a loss. Ceremonies exist for a reason. To mark time.

On graduation day, a temperate morning in June, our family walked to the park. Having lost all pretense and sense of decorum, I wore flip-flops. I carried my suede pumps in my canvas tote with my vaccination card, camera, and lip gloss. Why after the pandemic any of us ever have to wear stilettos again is beyond me. We should burn anything with a heel like we did bras.

The metal fold-out chairs were broiling in the sun. I used the regal blue-and-white commencement program as a fan like some Tennessee Williams character sitting on her porch in August complaining about the humidity. We sat socially distant from the other parents, which meant a lot of lip reading and pantomime. But mostly waving. And regret that I hadn't brought sunscreen. Suddenly, the music began to play. The traditional brass melody signifying the end of a school era. We all craned our necks to get the perfect view of the procession of girls, two at a time, walking in a line toward the crowd. Blue gowns, blue caps, and bouquets of yellow roses. I saw my sweet daughter with a hint of makeup, a steady stride, and a cracked smile. And I broke down. I cried. I wailed. Quite unexpectedly. My body was convulsing, and my younger daughter tapped my arm as if to say, *Please stop, you're embarrassing yourself, me, Dad, and the entire human race.*

When your children are little, people pester you with annoying, trite sayings like *It goes by so fast* and *Enjoy it while you can—they'll be gone in a moment!* You're sleep-deprived, your breasts are sore and chapped from pumping, and all you do is stuff poop-filled diapers into a plastic Diaper Genie. But I am here to tell you, as a woman who scoffed at those clichés, they're absolutely true. IT GOES BY SO FAST! By the time my daughter turned eighteen, I was just beginning to get the hang of the whole mother thing! And she's leaving? NOW? "Wait, wait, wait, there's a very good college five blocks from the apartment!" You see, a child's life is measured by grades—preschool, nursery, kindergarten, elementary, middle, and high school. They are markers to help their still-developing frontal lobe prepare for each progression toward their future: college, jobs, relationships, an Acura, children . . . but there is nothing for the parents! They're looking forward, and we're looking back. I wanted to pull my daughter's gown and drag her toward me, screaming, *I need two more years!*

Let's not forget, for nearly a year and a half we were sequestered in our home because of Covid—talk about familial stunted growth . . . And during that time, the umbilical cord stump grew back! Strong and sturdy! When you put a group of guinea pigs in a cage, they tend to press up against one another next to the metal rails. That was us. A small herd of guinea pigs curled up on the sofa, letting our emotions drop like poop pellets. I wish we could freeze that time and my daughter could be a junior again and we could actually look at colleges in person instead of via virtual tour conducted by a robotic, animated student. Shouldn't we simply reboot the lost time? Pretend the past year and a half just didn't happen? That would make her a sophomore again. I'm fine with that. I don't care if she graduates from high school at age twenty-eight. In fact, we could go to college together! And this time I'd pay attention and not chase upperclassmen!

The night after graduation was the prom. Another milestone. In one week, enough milestones to build a milestone wall. My husband and I have no reference for prom (except an image of Sissy Spacek covered in pig's blood). I went to an all-girls boarding school (there wasn't an all-boys school in a hundred-mile radius), and my husband had chess club the night of his prom. Guess what he opted for?

My daughter and I hunted for a dress for months. That's the best part. A precursor to weddings. UPS boxes were delivered and then returned. She would purchase a hundred-dollar dress from some shop in Australia that would cost me about the same amount to return. I may be bawdy in talk, but I'm conservative by nature. I wanted my daughter to wear a long turtleneck sweater dress. In June. There were dresses online I wouldn't wear as a nightgown on my wedding night. I know, I sound like my grandmother. I should be wearing a waistcoat and buckled shoes, waving the Bible. I know it's hypocritical. I've been practically nude on late-night television, but I'm old. And when you're old, you've got nothing to lose. My daughter is young, and the stakes are much higher.

I hate shoe shopping. It's exhausting. And nobody has feet that are exactly the same size. I find searching for shoes requires a B12 shot, a PowerBar, and lots of water. And then to be the wingman for someone else shoe shopping? I just wanted to curl up in one of the empty boxes under the tissue and nap. My daughter tried on hundreds of pairs of shoes for prom. Until finally Cinderella found the perfect diamondy, strappy slipper. I had hit the wall, so when she announced she'd finally found the shoes, I snorted some smelling salts and threw down my credit card on the counter. However, in my haste to get through the store without being sprayed by Rihanna perfume, I didn't fully absorb the price of the shoes. Let's just say, at the price, there should have been real diamonds glued to the straps. Happy graduation, sweetheart! Hold on to these shoes forever—someday you'll be able to sell them and pay your rent!

I had wiped my tears on the arm of my husband's jacket several times during the graduation ceremony. When the headmistress called out my daughter's long and impossible-to-spell last name, she paraded across the stage with purpose and confidence.

I pictured a very specific memory. When she was two years old wearing a floral party dress, bare feet, and a con-cerned look. It was her birthday, and the backyard was filled with balloons and family members. She had trepidation about stepping down onto the grass and being consumed by the celebration and my mother-in-law's insatiable appetite for photos. (She carries a $8^1/_2$ x 11 plastic grandchildren brag photo book with her everywhere.) My daughter took in the balloons, her name being sung off pitch, and the lavender cupcakes with gold sprinkles, and threw her arms around my neck. "I just want to be with Mama," she whispered.

I peeled her off me and enticed her (with gummy worms) to join her party. But she never released her grip from my skirt.

And here I was, watching this grown girl marching into her future, and all I wanted was for her to break rank, throw her arms around my neck, and whisper, *I just want to be with Mama!*

Friends

The pandemic was like a huge flour sifter for our social lives. A way to siphon out the light and flaky and grasp onto the more substantial. Something happened when the humans were put in solitary confinement. Of course, the animal world flourished. They were not polluted, hunted, or trapped. Dolphins leapt in crystal blue waters, foxes scampered openly down main roads, bears rummaged furiously through garbage cans in daylight like women at a Neiman Marcus sample sale. I used a visceral strainer to preserve the relationships I held sacred and release the ones that seemed extraneous or owed me money.

I discovered that when the world calmed down and daily routines were reduced to washing and drying, an overabundance of friends suddenly seemed unnecessary. It was yet one of the many superfluous plates that spun in the prepandemic air.

You can blame it on age (and all that Mary Oliver poetry I read on Instagram), but the pandemic caused me to re-evaluate my social existence. I found I lost the appetite for chitchat. It's not snobbery. I don't feel more or less than, it's just a matter of how I want to spend my energy. It's a connection to empathy, kindness, depth, and a wider sense of altruism. And in its most base form—in with the good, out with the bad. And by "bad," I mean assholes.

I used to say yes to everything. Any invitation was met with "How fun, we'd love to!" Paperless Post? Check attend! Even though on our way to any soiree my husband would start strategizing how to exit before dessert. And make sure the car wasn't blocked so we could escape quickly, like we were going to fling open the doors with a piece of modern art over our shoulders. I never felt like time was precious or recognized that how I spent it had an impact on my mental health. Which is partly why I'm immature. And can't quite fathom my actual age. It wasn't until lockdown that I realized I was depleted from suppressing social anxiety. I could no longer attend a second cousin twice removed's destination fortieth birthday party. I had to stop speaking at the plethora of charity events for diseases I had to Google. I couldn't eat one more stale roll or wilted salad.

Looking at the ancient understanding of tribes, they have "very simple social structures with less stratification, which are held together by marriage, friendship, decency, and common interest. The basic integration mechanism of such associations is kinship with no economic class differentiation" (www.hierarchystructure.com). During the pandemic, our contemporary tribes were either born or regenerated. The current vernacular is "pods," but they're tribes. We pulled together nearby family and close friends and created our own ecosystem. An ecosystem that survived on Amazon and FreshDirect.

Other tribes were born from text feeds. There was my birth family text tribe—parents, brothers, sisters, their spouses, and so on. These were the daily health check-ins and debating of scathing op-ed pieces. An occasional photo, but there wasn't much to capture on film. My mother's thriving vegetable garden was a highlight. And there were friend-group tribes. These were pretty anemic until things started opening up and there would be an occasional snap of someone actually smiling or a child in a pool or lake or some representation of normality. There was always one person in each thread who posted every doomsday news alert, accompanied by a graph of soaring Covid numbers. I became pretty good at defusing them, inquiring what they'd made for dinner (cue the goat cheese lasagna photos) or sending a meme of a cat and a golden retriever napping together. We knew the news. We knew the numbers. The purpose of these texts was spiritual harmony, guys.

And when a new show dropped on HBO Max, it was as

if the threads received a collective shot of pure adrenaline. *Mare of Easttown* was particularly exciting. It was as if we knew Mare (Kate Winslet) and it was all happening in real time in our real lives. (On a side note—does every successful murder show have to include a missing dead girl? Is there no other hook? Do all studio notes say, "We love it, but can you just throw in a dead girl? Ideally a naked one?" "Sure, but this is a musical comedy.")

People had all kinds of reactions to the pandemic. I equate it to senility. Doctors say when a person reaches the depths of dementia, their true colors are revealed. The hysterics became hysterical, the depressed become morose, the deniers more defiant. One fearmonger turned into Chicken Little, emailing her catastrophic imaginings to her entire contact list. On the other extreme, a friend in denial couldn't quite comprehend that ordering a bouncy house for her kid's birthday party when we were still spraying toxic cleaners on all of our groceries was unconscionable. I focused on being resilient—for my family as much as for myself. And when I was full of despair, I kept it between myself and a box of Mallomars.

After I recovered from Covid, I couldn't help deliberating about who'd reached out and who hadn't. It might sound petty, but then I had never been in a life-threatening situation in a vacuum of unknowns. It was a tiny window into the dreaded fantasy of who would be there on my deathbed. Or who would show up to my funeral. And not just for the buffet.

The first couple weeks of the illness I was so delirious the Pope could have blessed me with holy water and I wouldn't have remembered. My husband received all incoming calls and provided a detailed report of my oxygen levels and eating habits. So it surprised me to hear that my close friend Patty hadn't checked in with him. It wasn't a secret that I was infected with Covid. Patty didn't have to send me a bouquet of balloons with a teddy bear or a crappy box of chocolates, but not a phone call or even a text? I tried to push these emotions aside. It was a global pandemic. Maybe she was stuck under her car? Or had left the country and was growing papayas in Belize? But the truth was, she couldn't handle it. Patty was one of a handful of people who was simmering with anxiety to begin with, popping Klonopin during the day and dangerously close to a full bottle of wine at night. So when the pandemic hit, she froze. She emotionally atrophied.

Then there were friendships destroyed by the contagion. Lucy, who was always forgetting her mask, had gone to her friend Martha's to borrow a vacuum cleaner. There was nothing else to do but clean and organize during lockdown, so if you had a broken vacuum or were out of sponges, you were in dire straits. Lucy's puppy had chewed the cord of her vacuum. She whizzed into Martha's with her hand over her mouth. "Oh, shit, I forgot a mask." Apparently, the two women were so elated to have human contact they stood in the foyer for an hour holding each other's hands while Martha tried to instruct Lucy on how to touch up her roots with shoe polish.

As it turns out, Martha had Covid (she was asymptomatic) and gave it to Lucy. When Lucy found out, she flew into a rage. She even talked about suing Martha. She was so unforgiving their friendship was destroyed and they no longer speak. I knew a girl in college who got herpes from a knowing boyfriend and she didn't get nearly that angry. My husband was asymptomatic when he gave me Covid. I don't blame him. But I weaponize it whenever I'm losing an argument.

And then there are the people who receded during that time. Allow me to recycle my bear comparison. If the bear were Covid. For some people, Covid (the brown bear) made them shout and make themselves very big, while others saw Covid (the black bear) and curled up into a little ball.

I had a serious boyfriend when I was in my twenties. We lived together and were later engaged. We hadn't had contact in about fifteen years. I thought about him, as I did all my exes, during quarantine, hoping that they and their families were healthy and safe. But for this one particular ex-love, the pandemic magnified how lost he was to me.

One afternoon toward the end of my recovery, I noticed an unfamiliar email address in my inbox. It was him. There was only one line on the email: *Are you dead?* he asked.

Yes! I replied.

And that was the only and last time I heard from him. Yet that exchange brought me immense comfort . . . He hadn't changed a bit.

Charades

Do I want to come over and play charades? That is a very loaded question. It's like being asked to come over and throw javelins. It's a skill. It requires a muscle that needs to be trained and honed and exercised. I had not played charades in about fifteen years. My fear was, I wouldn't be able to throw very far.

William Thackeray quipped that charades enabled "the many ladies amongst us who had beauty to display their charms, and the fewer number who had cleverness, to exhibit their wit." Being in my midfifties and the worse for wear from Covid (and mounds of ice cream), I had only my wit to exhibit.

But on the other hand, the invitation was extended to me by one of my mentors, Marlo Thomas. She is an exceptional woman. An actress, a producer, an activist . . . funny, warm, and extremely intelligent. Marlo created the album *Free to*

Be . . . You and Me, which informed my whole childhood. And along with which my husband danced and sang songs about boys wanting dolls and mommies in the workforce to our toddler daughters. Just to serve Marlo crackers and cheese would be an honor, let alone be an invited guest. On a game night!

So I'm lying on the sofa. My safe place. With a glass of seltzer and orange juice, bingeing the show *Damages*. As I've mentioned earlier, I had lost the will to shower, let alone go to parties; applying makeup was a thing of the distant past. So the idea of acting out an opera or a French movie title in front of a room of strangers seemed daunting. Not to mention the fact that my husband was working, so I would have to go solo. Alone on the drive there with all the nervous anticipation and then nobody to download with on the way home. And I was so comfy on the sofa. With my daughter's school fleece blanket swaddled around me. Our dachshund, Daisy, as a foot warmer underneath. Like I had been for the past year and a half.

But then that gut thing kicked in. That voice that whispers, *Are you here to watch* Damages, *or are you here to experience life?* Well, that was a toss-up. *Damages* did win many awards, and Glenn Close has never been more terrifically evil. But just saying the words "Marlo Thomas and charades" out loud sounds like a great *New Yorker* article.

It was this same little voice that pushed me to go on the

blind date with my (eventual) husband. To move to LA when I started my acting career. To adopt Cooper (even though I swore to my husband he would never grow to more than twenty pounds). So why would I allow a whiff of social anxiety and fear of the unknown thwart what could be an exceptional evening? And on that note, why am I afraid to try night clamming? But first, charades.

I texted Marlo, *I'm in!*

I typed the address into my GPS. It took me to a remote, unfamiliar cliffside area. More unknown. This was after a thirty-minute montage of what to wear to a charades party. You certainly cannot wear a dress for charades because if you play it the way I do, you need to be able to somersault, climb the wall, and fly spread eagle. I needed loose-fitting pants, a sweat-proof shirt, and comfortable shoes. If I was going, I was going for the gold.

It was the magic hour of dusk as I careened down a country road to the house. Turned the car off. Took a deep breath. There is something exhilarating about leaping into the unknown. I gathered up a bouquet of hydrangeas I'd picked from my garden. And walked down the path to the house.

It was a Cape Cod–style house with gray cedar shingles. As I approached the front door, I gasped at the vista to my right. This house, which felt like it was nestled in the woods, had a panoramic view of the water. Just water as far as the eye could see. No overly developed houses, no parking lots, no Starbucks. It was what I imagine Martha's Vineyard or Plymouth looked like a hundred years ago. Majestic and serene.

Marlo, petite and bubbly, hugged me and beckoned me inside. She was able to hold the hydrangeas with one hand, hand me a ginger ale with the other, and simultaneously introduce me to the splattering of guests over the jazz humming from the speakers. Oh, the house. I have to write about the house. Its bones, its vibe. The floor were large mahogany planks perfectly aged with years of red wine spills, dog paws, and perhaps a red wagon being pulled through the living room. The furniture had the worn look of generations of family members having sprawled all over them: linen-covered sofas that had seen many a shaggy dog, cup of coffee, and sandy foot. It was like walking into a *Twilight Zone* of a 1970s WASP summer house. A house where Susan Minot might have written a book or a Kennedy cousin lost a football on the roof.

I first noticed the actor Bob Balaban and his wife, Lynn Grossman. A friendly, brilliant couple who waved behind their mason jars of wine. The next guests to arrive were Alan Alda and his wife, Arlene. I heard his voice first. The very distinct voice of so many of my favorite movies, and, of course, the iconic *M*A*S*H*. I bit the inside of my lip to make sure nobody had spiked my scallops last night and I was in some altered state. And then . . . one of the most climactic moments of the past few years of my life . . . I saw Elaine May sitting on a sofa. ELAINE MAY! If you are too young to know who this master creator is—stop. Put this book down (just for a couple minutes) and Google all of the genius Elaine May accomplishments. And if you can find recordings of "Nichols and May," listen to all of them. You're welcome.

To be breathing the same misty, apple-cider-smelling air as Elaine May was beyond even my wildest dreams. As Sadhguru says, "Constantly seek that which you know to be the highest." And she is the highest. I tried not to stare. And by that, I mean I kept my eyes frozen on her and whenever she happened to glance my way, I would swiftly dart my gaze down to the floor. It was my "Beatles moment," or to-day, my "Harry Styles moment." How could I steal a piece of her clothing? Or maybe her margarita glass with a smear of her ChapStick?

Was there a way to bottle her DNA?

"Okay, okay . . . let's play!" Marlo clapped her hands. She elaborated on a list of the very specific and detailed rules of this particular charades game.

"We get it, we get it," Elaine shouted.

"Elaine, shut up!" Marlo barked back. She then turned to me, "I can talk to her like that; we were roommates!"

A jewel of a moment.

It occurred to me that this group of highly creative and

accomplished humans had been playing charades for years! This was their "thing"! I was witnessing history. And for a moment in time I got to step into it. I got to feel it, smell it, taste it, and have it be part of my own story. These were the peaks of one's life. Not the shiny celebrity patina, but the gathering of these creative and comedic minds. Minds that I have been enamored of all my life. In middle school I didn't want to dissect a frog, I wanted to dissect Carl Reiner!

Clap, clap, clap! "Okay, let's go!" Marlo raced around the room with a bowl filled with slips of paper. There were ones and twos, which would divide us into teams. I pulled out a two. Alan Alda and Arlene held their pieces of paper in the air. "Two! Who else is a two?"

I was a two, I was a two, I WAS A TWO!!!!!!! I danced over to them. Who else? Who else would join my dream team? Who else would hop on this unicorn and fly through the sky filled with fairy dust and gumdrops?

Alec Baldwin lumbered out of the kitchen, "I'm a two!" He's a surprise guest in this chapter.

The twos were the Aldas, Marlo Thomas and her husband, Phil Donahue, Alec Baldwin, and me. The Olympic team. I couldn't let them down. I couldn't let our country down.

One of the rules was you not only had to guess the clue given, but ultimately, had to guess the theme of the complete set of clues given by each player. No, these people weren't playing around. I mean, they were, but . . . I begged my mind to sharpen up.

My first pick was "Der Fuehrer's Face." How could I mask the fact that I had no idea if it was a film, book, TV film . . . I was frozen. I mimed "no idea" (shoulders shrugging). Was it a Hitler doc? I wanted to disappear into the big wooden planks of the floor.

They didn't get it. And I looked like an ass. By the way, it's a 1940s war song. A surge of humiliation engulfed me. My cheeks got hot. I was losing their confidence. I would make it up to them. I would be the world's greatest charades guesser.

I pulled up a tattered ottoman, my hands on my thighs, ready to pounce on any word association my tiny brain could glue together.

Alec's turn. He looked down at the piece of paper and smiled, then he took the stage in the lofty way only a man who'd played Stanley Kowalski could. I watched. Alec transformed. The film was guessed within seconds. A slight movement, a slight gesture, a slight expression was all an actor of his talent needed to have us jumping to a standing ovation. The other team was getting heated. Marlo ran for the bowl of scraps of paper. She tore one open and ran back to us, her ballet slippers scuffing across the floor. She was a pro. She didn't hesitate with how many vowels or second syllable. There was Marlo Thomas, with her big chocolate-doughnut-brown eyes and svelte figure in white jeans, miming a bicycle and pointing to various objects in the room, pulling her ear to summon us to scream, "Sounds like."

Phil Donahue was tucked into one of the sofas with a delightful smile on his face. When someone yelled out a word like "baby," it would spark him to sing, "That's my baby, no sir, don't mean maybe!" He was literally serenading us while some of the great comic actors of our time leapt around the room.

Elaine May was on the other team. One of the great sorrows of my life. I couldn't study her like an albino rhinoceros. I picked out of the bowl. It was one of Elaine's suggestions. I knew it because it was in green pen. She was the only one who had a green pen. I knew this because I had been tracking her from the second I arrived.

I stood up. Clasped my arms together like a giant mouth. "*Jaws*!" Alec shouted.

Yes. That was it. That was my three seconds working with the great Elaine May. But I can truthfully say that Elaine wrote something for me that I got to act out on a stage, right?

The evening went on, filled with plates of chocolates, wine, and wild laughter. Finally, all the scraps of paper had been crumpled and tossed on the floor. Charades was over. Group two won.

After ten o'clock, guests started gathering their sweaters and saying their goodbyes. I sat glued to my chair. I didn't want to leave. I didn't want to say goodbye; I wanted to play charades with this group for the next decade.

I held on to Elaine a little too long. She's petite and svelte and had to muster all her elbow strength to crowbar herself free. And I refused to release Alan Alda's hand. And Arlene Alda's hand. My dream was that they run down the sandy path and swing me up like a baby. I lost their grips when they stepped down the porch steps. And disappeared into the night.

I stood alone holding my cell phone flashlight. I could see Phil and Marlo through the window clearing glasses and napkins. All good things must come to an end. What a dumb saying. Just as I started my forage back to my car I heard, "Ali!" I started to tremble a little; had they realized I'd stolen the green pen? Marlo walked out to the porch. "You're a good player, Ali! See you at the next charades!" NEXT CHARADES! I was in! I'd made it!

The whole way home I thought about hiring a charades tutor, maybe taking a master class in charades. And as I took another deep whiff of the green pen, I thought—next time I will be on Elaine's team! Whether she likes it or not!

College

The only way to avoid emotional pain is to keep busy for as long as possible. At least that was what I learned from generations of my family who have continually pulled themselves up by their bootstraps. Until the pain became so full, it flooded, and they had to confront the damage. Or cork it. Or uncork it with alcohol. In which case it was hard to get the bootstraps up. I come from a long line of folks who inebriated themselves when life got tough. Hard cider was distilled to get through a winter of smallpox and to calm nerves during a mutiny on the *Mayflower*. I dislike the taste of alcohol intensely. Maybe a sip of fine wine or champagne for a toast (at my own wedding). But I never took to drink. When I'm stressed I usually take it out on sugared cereal or dark-chocolate-covered pretzels. Believe me, there are times when I wish I had a taste for whiskey or vodka. I'd love to be able to slap the table dramatically and announce, "God, do I need a drink!" And then make something that requires mint, grapefruit juice, and two kinds of liquor. I'd sip it slow and sexy to take the edge off. "The edge" meaning life, I guess.

My daughter was ten days from embarking on one of the biggest journeys of her life. College. She had done it. Worked hard, got in early decision to the college of her choice, and was ecstatic when the acceptance email popped up on the screen. There were lots of celebrations. Although I'm not entirely clear as to the purpose of all the hype. Wasn't that the point of the screaming matches to finish homework and the bald spots on the scalp from ACT self-doubt? The endgame was to get into college? I've never subscribed to the elitist, unbalanced notion that to be accepted into an Ivy League school guarantees a successful life. Every CEO and mogul I've ever met has told me that the most impressive people they'd hired had gone to undistinguished universities. I've always believed it's the person, not the crest. That said, my daughter got into the school of her choice and yes, I couldn't help but brag. The college swag and sweatshirts were bought, even the university collars for the dogs.

During the whole maddening application process, I had failed to confront the most salient detail, which was the fact that my eldest child would be leaving home. But you push that down, bury it deep as you try to bask in the reflective light of your child academically hitting it out of the park.

And make another trip to the Container Store. Polish off another pint of ice cream.

A few days (and six pounds later), it was almost liftoff.

The majority of boxes were packed and stored by the front door. What was left was a pile of tattered duffels from many past vacations (some still sandy on the bottom) that needed to be stuffed with her clothing to take her through fall and winter. The toiletries would need their own duffel. It seems you need a lot of serums in college these days. I think I brought a jar of Pond's and a toothbrush when I went off to school.

Then again, I drove myself to Bard in my used Honda Accord. There was never even a discussion about how I would get there. My parents never offered to take me. I don't remember Range Rovers and Subarus lined up in front of the freshman dorms as futons, lounge chairs, and floor lamps were paraded down the halls. I never went to Target or Bed Bath & Beyond, and Amazon didn't exist (Jeff Bezos was still in college himself). I never used a Pinterest board to help create my dorm room vision. I lugged a couple suitcases, some musty pillows, and a typewriter up the stairs myself.

As I helped my daughter prepare for her new life as a university student, I pored over pages and pages of emailed lists. Dorm needs: miniature fridge; high-back, spinal-support desk chair; drawer dividers and scented liners; and a mattress? I recall colleges provided mattresses as room and board. But as seems to be the case with everything today, nothing is ever enough. So I checked the boxes for everything a family of five moving into their new ranch house would need.

I was stuffing sock dividers (who knew they even existed and that people actually used them) into the side of a gigantic duffel when I noticed my daughter was blowing her nose and guzzling a bottle of Gatorade.

"You have a cold!"

"No, probably allergies . . . just sniffles." She was focused on the final leg of her goodbye tour as she followed her friends down the runway to the college liftoff. One by one, starting with the Southern schools, New York freshmen had cleared out. My daughter was simultaneously texting goodbye to one friend heading west to school and introducing herself to a student from Rwanda she had yet to meet.

Most of the packing was done, but there were still outstanding items on the checklist, like a haircut and new underwear. And more serums. She still had a runny nose. As she scampered down the street, I shouted, "Maybe you should get a Covid test!"

She stopped long enough to turn and roll her eyes. "That seems extra, Mom."

I was walking back from the market armed with turkey slices, mayo, and brioche. I was practically salivating at the vision of my impeccable sandwich with a pinch of sea salt and pepper, cut in half alongside a perfectly curated clump of bread-and-butter pickles. I would devour this at my kitchen table and scroll late-summer clothing sales to distract me from the well of emptiness into which I was preparing to fall. For months now, my daughter's looming departure had been a source of deep psychological pain; the first bite of my turkey sandwich would provide a momentary respite. That and a pair of jeans I had been coveting, at sixty percent off.

I could feel the vibrations in my pocket. The evil device I felt compelled to grab with every shake, ping, ring, and horn alert was not going to rule my life. I wasn't a teenager, for god's sake. But the vibrations kept up, and so finally I relented and swiped. A photo of my daughter's positive Covid test.

Now what? I felt like the wind had been knocked out of me. America had just pulled out of Afghanistan, a hurricane was destroying the shores of Louisiana, Covid numbers (even for vaccinated people) were rising rapidly. And along with all these uncertainties was the feeling of utter helplessness. Could we not count on anything anymore? My husband, younger daughter, and I (still clutching my brown bag of lunch goodies) all ran to local rapid Covid testing sites. And hundreds of dollars later we had all received negative results. Except the one person who really needed to be negative to stay positive.

We were on our phones, snapping at each other about CDC guidelines, arguing over whether contagion counted from first day of symptoms versus day of test. But no matter how much we cried, screamed, and stomped our feet, we all had to quarantine for ten days. Again. Although the last time quarantine lasted about two years.

My daughter lay alone in her bed staring at the ceiling. Her room was strewn with plastic storage containers and stacks of sweaters that had never made it into a suitcase. FaceTiming with her mother from the kitchen while she was upstairs held hostage in her room didn't seem to have the therapeutic effect I had hoped; apparently, it was "annoying" to watch someone else scarf the last pint of ice cream in the house while you weren't allowed to come downstairs yourself.

Everyone has their own reaction to quarantine. Just read the *New York Post*. Some people refuse to do it; some people are enraged by it. Some lie about it. And some lean into it. It's a forced time-out. By law, I have to stay in my house, watch *Dexter*, and eat cereal for dinner. More important, I can be with my family uninterrupted by the cacophony of life. This is not to say I don't hate the circumstances that led us there, and grieve the lives lost during this horrible time. But I'm keenly aware of how quickly children grow up, and would be lying if I didn't confess that I found consolation in having had them under my roof for a little longer.

Leading up to our lockdown, I was having nightmares about separation. I would wake up in a sweat, images of my daughter as a baby in a ruffled sun hat playing in the sand, painting seashells and getting her face painted for the first time playing in a loop in my head. The dreams were like Super 8 clips of the past. First steps. First birthday cake. First day of school.

But here's the thing—separation is difficult even in conventional times. There is no reference point, no guide, for a mother and daughter spending nearly two years in lockdown and then being wrenched from each other's arms.

The second night of quarantine number two, I poured myself a glass of prosecco. Remember when I said I never took to the drink? "There comes a time in every woman's life when the only thing that helps is a glass of champagne," Bette Davis supposedly said. I just wanted to numb. Why couldn't I drink booze like a normal person? How hard is it to down a couple shots of whiskey? I took a sniff of the whiskey in our liquor cabinet and almost threw up. I uncapped the tequila bottle. Maybe on ice cream? But some points in life can't be dulled by booze. Or pills. Or Milk Duds. Sometimes you just have to square your shoulders and head straight into the storm.

The irony was, those ten days ended up offering a therapeutic respite from all our anxieties and fears. And my daughter and I were able to process them together. What if she didn't make any friends? What if she hated college? What if I didn't like any of her friends? What if I loved college? We played out every scenario. For ten days. And when the day came and quarantine was lifted and the car was packed, there was a sense of calm. We didn't have to armor ourselves from feelings by filling our time with frivolous errands. They sell maxi pads at the school bookstore. And we felt prepared. She was ready. Ready to embark on her new chapter. And, I thought, I was ready too.

College
Part 2

I could not stuff the Big Mac into my mouth fast enough. When I fisted a bunch of fries in along with it, I nearly choked. We had stopped at a service station somewhere in eastern Connecticut. Pathetic? I didn't care about the optics. I had just tearfully hugged my daughter in front of her ivy-covered college dorm and driven away. Like a scene from a real tearjerker. Think *Cast Away*, with my daughter as Wilson the volleyball. When I saw the yellow arches in the distance it was like the North Star was guiding me. I may or may not have crossed two lanes of traffic as I peeled off the exit.

When we took my daughter out for breakfast that morning I had only been able to manage a mug of lukewarm tea. Everyone else had had pancakes. My stomach had been in knots. And yet, after the wrenching goodbye I was suddenly famished. But no amount of special sauce could fill the aching emptiness inside me.

I tried to sort through my feelings as I sped south on 95. Why the doom and gloom? My daughter was going to college, not strapping into a rocket ship with Elon Musk.

As I cruised by yet another Cracker Barrel restaurant, it hit me—I was not done parenting my daughter. I still had some stories to tell, life lessons to imbue, and cookies to bake.

I was fourteen when I was dropped off at boarding school. And that was that. I came home on vacations and breaks, but after the age of fourteen my room at home was merely a museum of my childhood. And over the years, my possessions slowly disappeared, given to charity or tossed. And my room became an antiseptic guest room.

Fourteen is a very young age to venture out into the world. I like to say that boarding school was my *Orange Is the New Black*. It was all about survival. I started smoking (Kools) to fit in and fly under the social scrutiny radar. Every day was about making it through to lights-out. I don't recall European history debates or a riveting paper on *The Scarlet Letter*. My greatest education came from experiences, not textbooks. If I learned anything, it was from two seminal events.

I was a sophomore living in a dorm with a kleptomaniac,

a nymphomaniac, and a hypochondriac. How's that for a sitcom! An upperclasswoman had broken into the dean's office with a screwdriver the night before exams and stolen the carbon ink sheets for the tests. This was back in the day, when you printed off one master inked template. It was my school's Watergate, and Mallory, a senior who wore a faded purple sweatshirt with the word "Cocaine" stitched across it, was our G. Gordon Liddy. The stolen exams were copied and sold. At two in the morning there was a knock on my door and a senior, smelling like stale cigarettes and desperation, crept in and offered me a copy of the chemistry exam. She was like a drug dealer, whispering and darting her eyes back and forth from the door to me.

"Come on, come on . . . you want it or not? It's a clean copy."

My heart was pounding. A pivotal moment. It was one of those moral dilemmas I assume they teach at Bible camp.

I declined. Not because I was so high-minded and righteous, but because I had studied hard for the exam. I'd made note cards and sat in the library with Katherine, who excelled at science and whom I wasn't particularly close with, and we'd quizzed each other relentlessly. Believe me, all I'd wanted was to be in the student lounge with a half box of cold pizza watching *General Hospital*. But I bit my fingernails to the bone and memorized the periodic table of the elements. So to be offered a bike when I had trained for the marathon seemed like a waste. The senior disappeared into the dark hallway, off to prey on another tenth grader who was driven to exceed her parents' monumental expectations.

A few days later, the metaphorical sirens were blaring, helicopters circling, and guns pulled. One by one, students were pulled into an interrogation room by the disciplinary committee. Finding the culprits was the institution's top priority. Arguably, their efforts would have been better served hiring a therapist to treat the rampant eating disorders, but their sights were trained exclusively on Examgate.

One by one, students, ashen-faced and shaky, were released from the room. Some in tears because they either ratted on their friends or were suspended. And then the head of the ring, Mallory, walked out wearing dark sunglasses. She had been expelled.

Mallory was being escorted out by two teachers and her parents when she spotted me across the quad. I was walking to class in a Lanz nightgown over sweatpants and a down coat. A knit hat on my head, carrying a bunch of textbooks. She stopped. And screamed at the top of her lungs, "Fuck you, Ali Wentworth, fuck you!" Everyone turned to stare at me as she was led to her dorm to pack her things. I was horrified and terrified. Not to mention mortified.

For the longest time I could not figure out what the vitriol was all about. Why me? Why was I singled out? Maybe I represented the other choice. I didn't participate in a criminal act. A circumstance that had left her expelled from high school, brought humiliation to her parents, and faded her cool-girl status. Or maybe I happened to walk by at the wrong time.

Twelve girls were expelled. It was a bloodbath. And it rocked the community and scared it straight. Do I remember my paper on how Scout was the voice of a new generation in *To Kill a Mockingbird*? Not really. Do I know that I can trust my gut and make a good decision? Well, in this case, yes. I'm no saint and made some idiotic choices (and still make them on a daily basis), but I didn't get myself expelled from school. And they don't teach that in textbooks!

The second thing I learned in boarding school is that humans love who they love! I know, a bumper sticker, but in its simplicity lies truth.

I grew up in a little cashmere box. I saw the world through the eyes of *The Brady Bunch*. A football could break your nose and cause you to miss prom, any problem could be rectified in twenty-two minutes, and the fundamental relationship in life was between a boy and a girl. Or a man and a woman. Or a housekeeper and a butcher.

The 1980s saw a dramatic rise in the awareness of gay rights, but not in the elite, New England enclave in which my school was nestled. If there were lesbians in the dorms, they were hidden deep in their walk-in closets. Sadly, it was not something that was readily nurtured and accepted. In fact, sometimes it felt like the Salem witch hunt as mean-girl cliques openly speculated who was or might be gay.

I escaped a lot of girl drama in the art room. It was loft-like, with huge windows. It smelled of turpentine and coffee. Mr. and Mrs. Shatterly taught all the art classes. Mr. Shatterly had a mustache that reeked of Camel cigarettes, and he carried a ceramic mug of coffee everywhere. The inside of the teal-colored mug was stained dark brown from years of built-up coffee residue. Mrs. Shatterly had magnetic blue eyes and silver streaks in her dark hair, which was always brushed back off her weathered face. They were the only version of parents I had at school. She taught me techniques for painting glass and silver in elemental still lifes. He pressed me to be more abstract and bolder with color. The safety of the art sanctuary was so comforting to me, I considered being a professional artist and applied to college as a painter. But, in the long run, I went with a much safer choice: acting.

I remember the day. Crisp and cold. The kind of weather that required layering a turtleneck sweater under the aforementioned Lanz nightgown and down coat. And the kind of morning, with its frosty dew, that made it too unforgiving to run across the soccer field to the commissary for Fruity Pebbles. Breakfast cereal came in miniature boxes, and when you were late for class, you cut a cross into the box, filled it with milk, and used it as a carry-out bowl.

Our dorm mother asked me to come into her living room. I sat on the stained sectional and watched her feed her toddler Doritos and Diet Pepsi. For breakfast.

"I got something hard to tell you," she stated, shoving a Dorito in her mouth.

"I know you love Mrs. Shatterly . . ." She paused, clearly searching for the right words.

I nodded.

"Well, she's gone."

"What do you mean, gone?"

"She's not dead. She's gone. She left." She tossed another chip into her mouth. My dorm mother clearly did not want to have this conversation.

"I don't understand?"

She finally made eye contact with me. "Mrs. Shatterly has run off with Lisa Dunn."

I sat there like I was trying to solve a complicated calculus question.

"Lisa Dunn . . . the senior?"

"Yes."

"Run off where?"

"I don't know where; they're *together*, together. It's so . . . Anyway, she's gone. Mr. Shatterly will take over her classes."

In the pre-#MeToo culture, the revelation of a teacher-student relationship was fairly ho-hum, but the fact that Mrs. Shatterly and Lisa were both women was hard for me to wrap my head around! I simply had no context. When I was growing up in Washington, DC, in the 1980s, a majority of gay people were closeted. And had worked for Reagan. After their affair broke, more and more of the girls at school began discussing same-sex relationships. A few of my friends confessed they were lesbians. And it was such a release. To talk about it. To understand and embrace it. To work toward normalizing it. Mrs. Shatterly and Lisa moved to the suburbs of Berkeley, California, and (as far as I know; it never appears in the alumni magazine) are still together.

I lay facedown in my bed willing myself not to FaceTime my daughter. She was probably out to dinner with a group of intellectually curious young women in jeans and ripped sweaters deciding which feminist history course to take. Her mind will be nourished by cerebral professors and famished TAs. And everything else will come from life. I have my stories. I have my experiences. And all of them, the good, the bad, and the ugly, have led me to this moment. There are some things I can't teach her. I administered Children's Tylenol, rubbed her back when she was sad, surprised her with cinnamon toast in the morning. I helped nurture this beautiful wildflower. And now she needed to grow on her own, soaking up the earth's nutrients and basking in the sun's warmth.

But that doesn't mean I can't still bake her cookies. And FedEx them.

The Runner

It was September, although given the mugginess and stench of the city, it felt like mid-July. My husband had returned to being in studio, so we ventured back to the city, our home, for good. Manhattan had been ravaged by Covid. But as diehard New Yorkers, we were determined to support the city every way we could. Even if that meant hopping over puddles of urine in the subway or dining outside next to a jackhammer and a flooding rain drain. I was grateful that Covid numbers were going down and praying our city could build itself back up.

Central Park is my refuge. I know all the paths leading up and around the loop in Harlem. I know the hours Stanley plays his saxophone under the bridge leading to the Great Lawn, and I know the areas to stay clear of in the Ramble (let's just say the rubber gloves strewn in the bushes are not from Covid precautions). Cooper has his sweet spots in the park too. Dogs are allowed to be off leash until nine a.m., and he utilizes that time to forage behind the dumpsters by the Loeb Boathouse and sniff out the dense rat population near the Belvedere Castle.

After months of tomato and mayonnaise sandwiches and more mint chip ice cream than I'd care to admit, it was time to seriously think about getting back to exercising. And no, walking up a flight of stairs did not qualify as "exercise." During lockdown, I could simply open a door and let the dogs run out howling and peeing simultaneously. But in the city, Cooper requires at least a five-mile walk a day. And to relieve himself by seven thirty a.m. I could be up all night dancing on a bar in my bra and chugging tequila, but at seven thirty a.m. the leash must be on and poop bags shoved in my coat pocket. Rain or shine. And as Cooper is a hound and a hunter, it's only fair to let him lead by his nose and enjoy a sense (and the scent) of freedom. We have a path, a method, a pace to our walk. Any morning at 8:20, you can practically clock the exact patch of grass we will be crossing. It starts at our apartment and winds through Central Park to the bridle path. The bridle path was originally created for horses, thus the name, but over the years it has become the mecca for all serious New York runners. And if the weather is kind it's filled not only with joggers but with dogs, baby carriages, and school children. My favorite time is winter, in the magical moments during a snowfall, when I usually share the path with one or two cross-country skiers.

I felt so sluggish. I resented my new paunch. All those fried clams had seemed like a good idea at the time.

Even Cooper was tentative about being back on concrete. As we made our way through the familiar terrain, Cooper left messages on all the trash cans and lampposts he used to frequent. Canine social media. Judging by the number of stops, he had a backlog of messages.

We had just started on the bridle path. I was already drenched in sweat. And Cooper was panting. Good Lord, we were so out of shape. He walked ahead of me but checked regularly to make sure I wasn't trailing too far behind—he knows I'm the one who feeds him. Suddenly, a runner appeared. A svelte woman in tight black leggings, gray bobbed hair, and sunglasses. Black Matrix-type sunglasses that blocked out any sign of eyes. Or humanity. She ran in the middle of the path right toward my dog. Now, she could easily have careened a few inches to her left or right to avoid my affable baby. But instead, she beelined for him, nearly striking him with her leg.

"Get your fucking dog on a leash!" she screamed.

I was startled back to the childhood moments when my mom used to bellow for me by my full name. Guilt and shame washed over me; I must have done something horribly wrong. But after conducting a swift mental review I realized I had done nothing wrong. My dog was allowed to be off leash on that path.

"Dogs are allowed to be unleashed until nine a.m.!" I shouted, but in a neutral tone, without rage.

Without even turning around, she extended her arm in the air and gave me the finger. She held it up for about ten seconds as she ran off.

A few people in the area had stopped. It had been jarring to them as well. Even if she had been in the right (and she was not), her vocal lashing did not fit the crime.

I looked around and saw there were many dogs running, jumping, playing, frothing at the mouth, liberating half-eaten bagels from the trash. Why single my dog out? And why so nasty? There was no reason to hit a ten on the temper meter when a three would have sufficed—that is, if you are the sort of person who feels compelled to shriek at a complete stranger.

This kind of moment can create a pall over one's whole day. It can start optimistically—watching a whimsical segment on *Good Morning America* about a bear cooling off in a swimming pool, receiving some heart emojis from a friend. And then out of nowhere, you run headfirst into someone else's rage.

As I gingerly kept walking (and Cooper almost beheaded a squirrel), I thought about the morning's shocking pivot point. Was she the exception, or just a symbol of the undercurrent of rage roiling our society? Have humans reached their capacity for simple dignity? Yes, it was New York, and that's part of the character of the city—a taxi driver flipping off a van that cuts him off or a super yelling up at a window washer who's dripping water on the awning; this is the soundtrack of the city. But what I had confronted wasn't an attitude; it was anger. A fury that once was tamped down under the concrete sidewalks had come shooting up through the cracks.

Our whole country was angry. You only had to open your computer to feel the heat of the fury.

This isn't a political diatribe. It comes from a sense of loss. Loss of community. A loss of kindheartedness. That morning I walked around the park feeling disoriented in a very familiar place. People eyed one another sideways, as if everyone was a criminal and knew their ATM pin number. Even dogs who used to savor sniffing one another's butts now just growled.

I too was filled with animosity. As the woman was hitting her stride on the other side of the reservoir, I started contemplating how I would seek my revenge. I would mobilize everyone in the park to create a human chain at the park exit and force her to apologize. I would tie a fishing line between two trees so she would trip, falling on her face in the muddy trail. And darker. I could tap so easily into the exact ire I was slapped with. I could hit level ten just as easily as a stranger who didn't want to move an inch to avoid kicking a dog.

Intellectually, I understood the source of the toxic undercurrent of our culture. The insecurity and fear of the unknown that translates so easily into outrage. But no amount of incisive op-eds or tweets can fix that. America needs couples therapy.

I put Cooper on the leash. What the hell, we were enervated, and it wasn't like he was bounding over hills.

I saw her coming toward me. Those black sunglasses like oil slicks. My insides felt hot. I wanted to grab her by the shoulders and scream obscenities at her! For ruining my morning, for being mean, for not being a dog lover, for the Dow being down, for climate change, for my extra eight pounds, for ALL OF IT!

And when she was less than a hundred feet away, I called out to her. Kindly.

"Hey, thanks for the heads-up." I pointed to the leash and smiled.

"Have a great day!" I continued.

I watched her expression change in slow motion, not unlike a cartoon character's. She was confused. Baffled.

As we walked home, I thought to myself that maybe it was a step. Maybe we pause. Take a breath before we react.

And just maybe, the next time we see each other, she will take a breath and wave.

Generation Gap

It's a strange shift when you become a parent to your parent. The people you used to fear upsetting and disappointing suddenly become these vulnerable people who need your guidance and wisdom. And you no longer have to hide the scent of cigarettes on your breath. It's an abstract version of *Freaky Friday*.

For me, it's very hard to see my parents as frail. Perhaps because, deep down in the bowels of my psychological DNA, I still need their approval. But I think it's more likely that I simply don't want them to ever die.

When I had Covid, I was hit with a sense of mortality, certainly. It wasn't that I thought I was going to die so much as the tragic death toll we were witnessing on a global scale. I have a visualization trick I fall back on when I find myself feeling panicky about the fragility of life. And it's this: I am a tiny speck on an asteroid flying through space—a speck with no significance whatsoever. I am a blip. And this actually makes me feel better. I am nothing, and nothing matters. Hallmark should hire me.

And when it comes to ego and the quest for immortality through your work? I remember gushing about the amazing Mary Tyler Moore, whom I worshipped, and whom my daughters had never heard of. It's all fleeting. Even if I won three Oscars and two Golden Globes, decades from now nobody would remember. One decade. I can't even remember who won an Oscar last year. However, I'd still like the experience of holding the statuettes and sitting on Ryan Reynolds's lap.

Like so many people my age, I am sandwiched in that time between aging parents and children beginning to soar. And it is a painful heart tug in all directions. Being a mother to my daughters, being a mother to my mother.

And right in there, toggling between flipping through senior living catalogues and booking flights to see my daughter at college, is the inherent struggle: to be the rock.

I don't believe in parenting books. There is no formula, no one-size-fits-all. You do the best you can with the children you have, with the person you're raising them with (if there is another person involved), in the circumstances you live in and the era into which you were born . . . Some of the most extraordinary people I know came from the worst of circumstances or were unloved, and yet these emotional hardships can shape some of the most empathic and phenomenal humans. Chris Rock said his experience with bullying was "the defining moment of my life . . . it made me who I am." He even thanked the pack of boys who regularly "kicked my a—, spit in my face, and kicked me down the stairs," because the experiences not only helped him to think quickly on his feet, but also fueled his drive to succeed. That being said, you don't ever wish hardship on your children. I'm not dropping my daughters in the forest with a Swiss Army knife and a can of tuna to see if they find their way to safety. The tough-love school is not a natural fit for me.

As my children are set to sail, all I can do is love them from the sidelines and give the only advice I have. Whether it's met by deaf ears is up to them.

So to my daughter in college and my younger daughter close on her heels, I offer you this:

Slow and steady. Don't show up in a glitter halter top and roller skates just because everyone is vying to stand out. Stick with your hoodie and jeans. You will eventually be seen. By your people.

Don't judge your roommate. They are more interesting than you think, even if—*especially* if—they're from a place you've never been. And they will be your best friend the first three weeks. You will cling to each other, primarily so you won't have to eat alone in the dining hall. Never forget that shared purpose, and treat them with kindness, even if you go your separate ways.

When you go to parties, get a plastic cup of club soda and cranberry juice, vodka, your choice (and never let the cup out of your sight), but don't get so drunk that you aren't in control. And you vomit on a stranger. Or yourself. Be the one they vomit on.

I realize that sex is part of the college culture like pizza in Milan. But don't eat more than one pie a night!

You will never have the luxury and time to be educated this freely again. Take the class on gender and public policy or the intellectual history of exile. If you want to be a lawyer, take a painting class, and if you want to be dancer, take a physics class.

Join the clubs and sororities and fraternities if you feel inclined, but don't be defined by them. And reach out to the people who don't run in your pack. Even though we, as humans, are most secure in a tribe, there is so much to learn from other tribes, and that is how we expand our minds. And make better fashion choices.

Lean into the discomfort. You are growing and expanding, which can feel thorny and graceless, but I promise the muscles you can't see are strengthening. Contentment doesn't make you grow; discomfort does.

Take a moment to lie in the grass, hike up the mountain, jump in the lake, learn that metro system. Wherever your college is, be part of the ecosystem. And please wear a coat. Even if you're a sexy witch for the twerk-or-treat Halloween party.

—

My mother always gifted me such sage advice. "Don't let the wolf in the door." (Still not exactly sure what that one means.) "When you're depressed, close your eyes and think about Christmas." And now I'm the person who doles out guidance. I think I will always feel like the child no matter the circumstances, but there's something satisfying in giving a little bit of wisdom back. I quote Rita Mae Brown to my mother: "Dying's not so bad. At least [you] won't have to answer the telephone."

My mother is the strongest, most formidable person I have ever known. She is accomplished, yes, but she is a force who is always true to herself and has an impact on everyone she meets. My mother can curtsy before the Queen of England in a Givenchy suit and feathered hat as easily as dig holes for tomato plants in her garden in rural Maine.

I have revered her all my life. I've always wanted to be her when I grew up. And now I've grown up. And she's eighty-six years old.

To my spectacular, maturing mother, I offer you this:

Walk. Move your body. You need blood flow and muscle, or you won't be able to get to the post office or pick blueberries. And don't you want to go to the outlet mall with me? (Note to self: move your body too.)

Hold on to your women friends. As long as you can. Because one day they're all dead. (You actually told me this; I'm recycling it.) It is your women friends who hold the oral history of your life.

Be in control of your finances for as long as you are of sound mind, and then legally put someone you trust in charge. Maybe somebody outside the family. But not the guy who mows the lawn.

Surround yourself with beauty, even if it's just a mason jar of wildflowers. But when the flowers are decaying and the vase water smells like eggs and sewage, it's okay to throw them away.

If you have to take Norvasc for blood pressure, take it with a Klondike bar.

Remember your stories. Pass them on. Particularly any salacious affairs.

You get to be the crazy old lady now! Take advantage of it! Yell at bratty kids, scream at the geese that shit on your lawn, tell the grocer he should give you the bruised apples for free . . .

Label your medications. Label your medications. Label your medications.

Tell me your secrets. I know you have them.

There's no reason to yell at the television. I swear, they can't hear you.

You don't have to get out of your nightgown . . . but you really should.

No, you cannot get a puppy.

Keep being curious. Keep reading books and being inquisitive about the world. (I promise I'll get to the Eleanor Roosevelt biography you sent me. It's just so many pages!)

And last, no, you're not driving. Anywhere.

Soon the generational Wheel of Fortune will spin again. And the arrow will point to me. And I will hold on to all the judiciousness of my mother and be grateful for my daughters, who will cradle me. I hope when my children find themselves straddling the fence of caring for their children and for me, they will build upon the foundation my mother and I have provided. And that they will pass the blueprint on to their children.

The
Final
Chapter

My stepfather died during Covid. Not from the virus itself. In his sleep and quite blissfully. Louis was ninety-nine years old. My mother pleaded for him to hold on till one hundred, but he decided that was too many candles. And he was ready.

Boy, had he lived! He was a sailor, a skier, and an academic, and he loved dirty jokes. Louis had lived every second of his full life, which is why his death wasn't filled with anguish and grief; the tears were tears of reverence and love.

We had to wait for months to have a proper memorial. Months of waiting for closure. And finally, on an autumn day in Cambridge, Massachusetts, he was laid to rest. We gathered in a small church that was surrounded by headstones and statuaries of carved dogs mounted on slabs of marble, family monuments, and dedicated benches. A serene cemetery ("cemetery" in Greek means "sleeping place") amidst woodland gardens, reflection pools, and scenic overlooks. I was awestruck by its splendor. Until I came across a tombstone that had A. E. WENTWORTH carved on it. A chill went up my spine, though my older brother got a kick out of it. (No matter how old I get, my older brother will never miss any excuse to tease me. It's like the second we see each other we revert into kittens in a box.) If you've ever stumbled upon a tombstone with your name on it that wasn't part of a Halloween decoration, it's extremely eerie. And you cannot help but start thinking about eternity real estate. That A. E. Wentworth had scored big in terms of plot size and placement.

We had all safely gathered at the small church. Some from out west, some from down east, some from nearby, with our tears and admiration for Louis as well as masks, Covid protocols, and pandemic fears. After almost two years of separation. Each of us carrying the remains of the distress and oppression of that time.

After the service, I walked through the gardens, admiring the ornate tombstones with carved angels and mausoleums with Celtic crosses. I hadn't thought much about the afterlife. Or the nonexistence thereof. And there I was with my widowed mother and fully grown siblings. It occurred to me that before long, I would be up at bat.

And then, like a bar mitzvah montage, I was flooded with memories.

When I was five years old, we lived in a big brick house covered in ivy at the end of a street surrounded by woods. At night the trees were spooky; you forgot that you lived in the center of a city. It was early evening on Halloween. My older siblings were out trick-or-treating. And I was home. My stepfather had dressed up as a tiger. Not the caliber of costume you'd see in *The Lion King*, but better than a plastic Walmart one. He crept down the stairs growling and holding up his polyester paws. "Offer the tiger candy?" my mom suggested, nudging me toward him. I remember holding the wooden bowl of mini chocolate bars and popcorn balls and shaking so hard I almost dropped the bowl. My heart was pounding. It was my first experience of real terror. I had never been so close to a tiger before.

I'm not sure why that memory is so vivid. Perhaps because it was a time of innocence, when I truly believed that my stepfather was a real tiger (who wore tasseled loafers). Maybe that kind of magical thinking doesn't exist in my psyche anymore. Like when my daughters were young and we would build a fairy village near my mother's house in Maine, deep in the mossy woods. And they believed in those fairies! We sometimes waited hours for their twinkling wings to appear. And a part of me believed they would.

I want to believe in wondrous things again. Perhaps we've been so beaten down by the global pandemic, raging partisan politics, and the realization of what we've done to the planet that the light at the end of the tunnel has dimmed. But I miss guileless joy and fantasy. I want to keep making gingerbread houses and catching fireflies in mason jars and making homemade love cards. There shouldn't be a cutoff age for dressing up.

It was still warm out, and the trees were just beginning the transformation to fiery oranges and reds. A few leaves had fallen on the grass. I thought about hot apple cider. And the fact that even if I was alone, I was going to carve pumpkins this year. And buy bulk candy with the mini boxes of Milk Duds.

My mind jumped to a time in Los Angeles when I was in my twenties. I was living up in the Hollywood Hills. And it was my best friend Michelle's birthday. I wanted to do something fantastic for her! She's one of those givers who doesn't understand the "take" part, so you have to shove birthday cake down her throat or use blackmail to get her to celebrate herself. There was a house next door to mine for sale. A much bigger modern white house nestled into a hill. It had been for sale for a couple months. I once saw a real estate agent showing Matt Damon the place. I ate my whole breakfast peering out the window spying on Matt Damon walking around the perimeter of the house. I should have invited him over for waffles.

And suddenly, it hit me. I would throw Michelle a surprise party! In that empty house! I sent out invitations. I hired a caterer (I needed tables and chairs) and food. Thank God, the water was still on in the house. The electricity was not; the whole party was lit by candlelight. It was otherworldly. And I had pulled it off. The next morning not a crumb could be found. I gave Michelle an enchanting party, and she was celebrated. But I also gave everyone a memory for the ages. It was not just any party, this was a party where the whole guest list could have been arrested for trespassing! I had the audacity to break into an empty home that did not belong to me and throw a birthday party! What if the police had driven by and noticed the suspicious activity? What if the real estate agent had clients who wanted to see the property at night? What if that client was Matt Damon? It wasn't that I was being mischievous, but I took a risk. I thought outside the box. And nobody has ever forgotten that night.

I walked down a small grassy knoll that led to more magnificent carved monuments. I looked back at my family walking in twos toward Louis's grave. My mother was arm in arm with my brother.

I stopped at a shrine of a husband and his beloved wife from the 1800s. I looked over at my husband. He had his arm around my older daughter. So handsome in his dark suit. So loving. I hadn't even thought about our final resting place. This is not a decision about spring break destinations or what historic tour to drag our children on. It's not even picking a temporary home. This choice is forever. Where do I want to spend eternity? My husband may want to be buried on a golf course. I have a horrific handicap, so that's not ideal for me. Plus, in the afterlife I want his full attention. Are people allowed to be buried on a public beach? I could see why people avoid the topic. I know I want to be buried next to him. Where that is? It doesn't really matter. I'll be with him. And he won't be snoring.

I thought about our wedding. The stress of venue and food and guest lists hadn't gotten to us. We just wanted to marry each other. Spend our lives together. Whatever ritual that determined our destiny was fine with us. Dance around a maypole? Fine. Vows in scuba gear? Sure.

When we walked into our reception hand in hand, husband and wife, I looked into my husband's eyes and said, "Let's have the time of our lives! Let's be in it so we can remember everything." Our first dance was actually our first dance. Our swift engagement hadn't lent itself to many club outings or ballroom events. The Greek band summoned every person, from my husband's ya-ya in her black lace veil to my college friend who was a sculptor and welder with long hair and a pierced nose, to join arms and shoulders and kick up their legs. And we danced hard. Late into the night, my husband and I went to our honeymoon suite in a romantic boutique hotel. He pulled off his tie, I kicked off my white satin heels, and we dove onto the bed. And twenty years later I remember in detail lying on the bed with him, my veil still attached to my head, sharing a cheeseburger in fits of laughter as we relived the best night of our lives.

—

When I returned home after the funeral I was hit with a bout of insomnia. Usually, when I'm hit with an unquiet mind I read a book or rewatch a Nancy Meyers film. But that night I stayed up looking through boxes and boxes of photographs. Pulling out film photos of my daughters with face paint, me pregnant, my youngest holding our fat dachshund as a puppy, my friend Michelle holding up granny underwear at my bridal shower, my husband and me in Cambodia gazing at Angkor Wat at sunset . . . I taped them to the walls of the bathroom. Because these are the windows of our lives. These are reminders of milestones and moments of joy and belonging. And there's room on the wall for more. Because no matter what little square of earth I'm buried in, these snapshots go with me.

Acknowledgments

Ah, the laborious, hair-pulling task of writing a book. Always a lonely quest. Just try doing it in a pandemic . . .

I have been lucky enough to have an editor, Jennifer Barth, who has the ability to scoop me up, clean me off, and steam me open (yes, more clam references). This is our fourth book together and I can't imagine working with anyone else. Always kind even when I miss deadlines, change artwork, and can't understand Microsoft Word.

To Jennifer Joel and the whole team at ICM: I am humbled to be in the company of your mahogany bookshelf of authors so beautifully displayed at your offices. Thank you, Jenn, for your honesty and integrity.

For Alyssa Mastromonaco: thank you for encouraging me after an early read. Gurl, you boost me up every day.

To all my friends and family who stayed connected with us during the awful dark days.

To all my girlfriends: you are everything!

Acknowledgments

To my husband, who read the final manuscript and only had a few notes.

To my daughters: I promise, there is nothing embarrassing about you in here. And if there is, I'll pay you off.

And to all dogs who are the greatest companions in good times and bad.

About the Author

ALI WENTWORTH is the author of the *New York Times* best-sellers *Go Ask Ali*, *Ali in Wonderland*, *Happily Ali After*, and *The WASP Cookbook*. She made a name for herself on the comedy shows *In Living Color*, *Seinfeld*, *Head Case*, and *Nightcap*, and as a regular on *The Oprah Winfrey Show*. Her film credits include *Jerry Maguire*, *The Real Blonde*, *Office Space*, and *It's Complicated*. She frequently guest-hosts *Live with Kelly and Ryan*, and hosts the Shondaland and iHeart-Radio podcast *Go Ask Ali*. She lives in New York City with her husband, George Stephanopoulos, their two girls, a hound mix, and an obese dachshund.